I0729748

New Media
in Art History

Régine Bonnefoit
Melissa Rérat
Samuel Schellenberg (Eds.)

NEW MEDIA IN ART HISTORY

// TENSIONS, EXCHANGES, SITUATIONS

DE GRUYTER

FOREWORD

Régine Bonnefoit, Melissa Rérat,
and Samuel Schellenberg

"Art History and New Media: What's Up?" was the title of the colloquium organized by the Swiss Association of Art Historians (VKKS-ASHHA-ASSSA) in collaboration with the Institute of Art History and Museum Studies at the University of Neuchâtel and the House of Electronic Arts (HEK, Basel/Münchenstein) in October 2021. The event was held in the most appropriate place in Switzerland to discuss such a topic, since the HEK is the Swiss competence center for art forms working with and in relation to new media and the latest technologies. The 2021 exhibition *Radical Gaming—Immersion, Simulation, Subversion*, in which sixteen artists disrupted the mechanisms of mainstream video games, raised some interesting questions that were discussed during the conference.

The colloquium brought together thirteen researchers from Switzerland, France, Germany, Austria, Great Britain, and the United States. In the spirit of transversal reflection, the aim was to probe the history of art in light of the evolution of so-called new media. From electronic to digital and then to postdigital, the techniques and practices included in this term pose both pragmatic and theoretical challenges to art history. The question "What's up?" in the sense of "What's happening?" refers to the current state of interaction between art history and new media. However, constant change and advances in the field of artificial intelligence, among other things, mean that today's new media will become the old media of tomorrow. The difficulty for art history is to keep up with the development of new media but also to recognize and use new opportunities offered by adopting a critical approach.

So, what's new? There are many different avenues of research, exchanges between the field of art history and new conceptual and technical tools, and a host of original projects that redefine and expand the thinking and undertaking of art history. This publication presents eight studies by eleven scholars working in different fields who explore the changes, opportunities, and tensions arising from the coming together of art history and new media. These articles develop selected considerations emerging from the conference, based around three axes, which have determined the organization of this book into thematic sections: "History and Historiography of Media"; "Use and Reception of New Media"; and "Creation, Conservation, Mediation." The scholarship herein is less an exhaustive assessment of the situation and more an interdisciplinary and international panorama of recent research.

Zsofi Valyi-Nagy kicks off the first section of this book by focusing on screenshots taken by Vera Molnar in 1974: images of two green-edged squares against a black background, which she programmed to be progressively deformed while considering the screen as an interlocutor in its own right. Valyi-Nagy points out the interrelations between art history and technology, underlining how transdisciplinary methodologies open up new research perspectives for new media art.

Fleur Chevalier paints a history of what she terms "cathodic art" in France. This neologism enables her to qualify the various experiments undertaken on televisual images by French artists between 1970 and 1990. She reconsiders the relations between and limitations of video art and television and the distinction between medium and media, and she unveils a little-known part of what could be called the "prehistory" of new media.

In her article, Katharina Brandl examines performances in digital, streamed games on platforms such as Twitch, where avatars can interact with each other and with the possibilities of the game mechanics. She investigates the question of whether it is possible to develop a perspective based on the history and theory of performance as a medium in the visual arts to conclusively allow for the inclusion of these recent artistic phenomena.

The second section, "Use and Reception of New Media," begins with an exploration of the quantification of aesthetic perception. Aline Guillermet shows that this enables us not only to track the human gaze but also to widen the possibilities for analyzing artworks and thus to exceed the capacities of the connoisseur's own eyes. After establishing the historical context of the issue, Guillermet underlines the limitations of quantitative approaches. To do so, she turns to several recent creations by artists who are active in the digital field, all of whom share the approach of putting the human being back at the heart of their work.

Nina Zschocke then provides a topical assessment of the current state of new media and its uses by sharing some experiences from contemporary art and research gathered since the beginning of the Covid-19 pandemic and, in so doing, calls into question our new digital life. By referring, for example, to the reflections and performances of artist Rory Pilgrim or to her memories as a lecturer, Zschocke illustrates how the digital world reshuffles the cards of private and public life. Her analysis concludes with a visual contribution by the artist collective U5.[1]

The last section, "Creation, Conservation, Mediation," concentrates on current projects that combine art history and new media resources. Sarah Amsler and Thomas Hänsli address data management in online thesauri and, more specifically, the translation of the Art and Architecture Thesaurus® (AAT®) in Switzerland, in which they were involved. The detailed presentation of this project, which reveals its history and ambitions as well as some Swiss subtleties, helps us understand the challenges at both a national and an international level.

Keyvane Alinaghi and Caroline Tron-Carroz teach open-source code for the preservation of digital heritage. They discuss a research project at the Ecole Supérieure d'Art et de Communication de Cambrai (ESAC) aimed at introducing students to digital tools, both current and supposedly outdated, and at raising their awareness of the history of media and technology.

Architects Dominik Lengyel and Catherine Toulouse explain their theoretical reflections and practical methods for creating virtual models of lost or only partially preserved buildings or ancient cities through a series of case studies. The visualization of stages of construction through virtual models remains an important method for archaeology, art history, and the digital mediation of cultural assets in museums and exhibitions.

Through their diversity, these contributions show the extent to which the question of the relationship between art history and new media remains open, constantly posed against the backdrop of rapid and relentless developments in the latter. Whether they are a tool, a material, or a medium, new media affect the field of art history. Today, it is almost impossible to practice art history without new media, whether in relation to the artists and works studied, to their conservation and dissemination, or simply to the daily practice of art history. And this is a good thing, since art history, as a field of the humanities, offers many resources to help each of us understand the increasingly digital nature of the professional and everyday world.

This volume was made possible thanks to the generosity of the Swiss Association of Art Historians, Articulations (Swiss Association for Young Art Historians), and the Institute of Art History and Museum Studies at the University of Neuchâtel. We would like to express our heartfelt thanks to the publishing house De Gruyter for the great opportunity and for the quality of its editorial staff; we are particularly grateful to Katharina Holas for the precise coordination of all stages involved in the creation of this book. We would like to thank Scribe Ltd. for the quality of its translation and proofreading work, as well as Elizabeth H. Stern for her copyediting and proofreading work. Our thanks also go to the director of the HEK, Sabine Himmelsbach, and to its curator, Boris Magrini, as well as to the Institute of Art History and Museum Studies at the University of Neuchâtel, the Swiss Academy of Humanities and Social Sciences (SAGW-ASSH), and the *Kunstbulletin* for their support in organizing the conference. And of course, we would like to thank the authors for trusting us with this editorial adventure. Without their enthusiasm and their in-depth knowledge, this publication would not have been possible.   //

1 See the website of the U5 artist collective, accessed March 18, 2023, https://u5.92u.ch.

HISTORY AND HISTORIOGRAPHY OF MEDIA

>>

#01

SCREENSHOTS FROM THE 1970s: VERA MOLNAR'S EXPERIMENTS IN INTERACTIVE COMPUTING

Zsofi Valyi-Nagy

In 1974, in Paris, artist Vera Molnar (born in 1924, in Budapest) used a mainframe computer to draw two perfect squares. Their outlines appeared in acid-green lines that glowed against the dark screen of the computer monitor. Molnar's choice of this geometric shape was not arbitrary. Her squares opened up an art historical dialogue with Albrecht Dürer's magic square, an emblem of art intersecting with science, and Kazimir Malevich's black square, the "zero of form," a point of origin for modern abstraction. Molnar's squares also gave a nod to the visual perception studies in which she was immersed that favored the square for its horizontal and vertical lines and its right angles. Finally, the square was one of the simplest forms to generate and manipulate computationally, since early computer graphics were best equipped for drawing geometric shapes. Molnar's computer drawing brought this icon of twentieth-century abstract art into dialogue with the century's most iconic machine: the computer.

But her gesture did not end there. Molnar used the computer to manipulate the squares, giving it instructions to displace each corner of the squares until their forms were no longer recognizable as squares. By making slight adjustments to the parameters of her program, she made the two squares twist and turn, converging and diverging in a sort of pas de deux. Molnar selected a handful of these images to appear in one

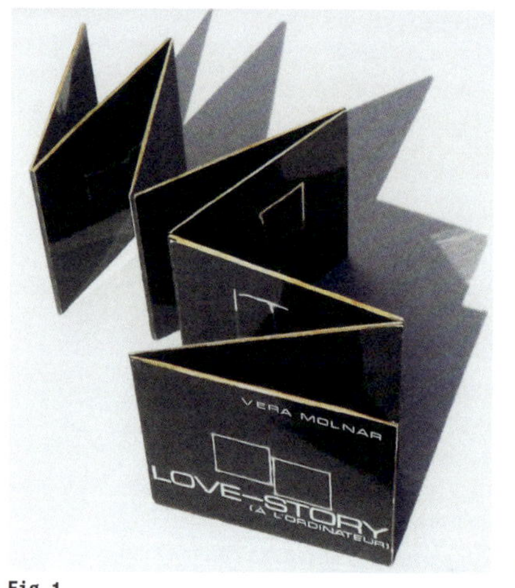

Fig.1

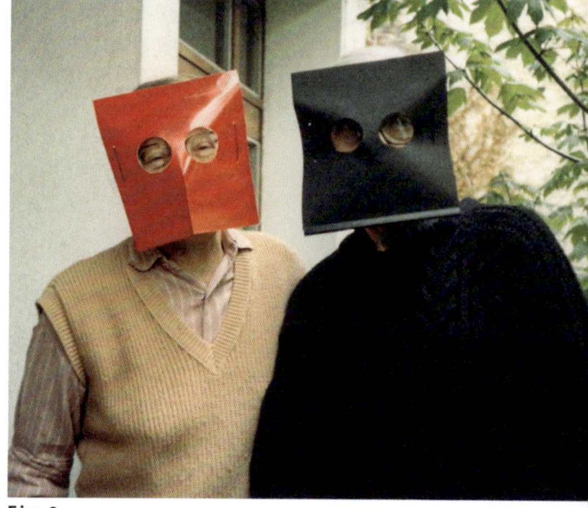

Fig.2

of her earliest artist's books, *Love-Story (à l'ordinateur)* ^{Fig.1}, which she described as a "computer-picture book" and a "livrimage," a portmanteau of *livre* (book) and *image* (picture).[1] *Love-Story* includes no text other than its provocative title, which anthropomorphizes the squares and invites a narrative reading of the images. The rumpled corners of the squares seem to gesture like hands, reaching toward one another. The squares bend in and out of shape, bowing and spinning around each other like dance partners. The shapes twist, tangle, and intertwine. The two squares are the same but different, cut from the same cloth but behaving differently, sometimes erratically, but never leaving each other's side.

Whose love story is this? One interpretation might be that the two squares represent the artist and her husband, François Molnar (1922–93), her lifelong interlocutor and collaborator ^{Fig.2}. François, who met Vera at art school in Budapest during the Second World War, stopped painting around 1960 and devoted himself to experimental psychology research, becoming an expert in eye movement and studying how the gaze moves around a work of art. The Molnars' practices were divergent but intertwined, mutually influential and always bearing traces of each

Fig.1 Vera Molnar, maquette for *Love-Story (à l'ordinateur)*, 1974, artist book, photographs mounted on cardboard, accordion fold with eight leaves, 14.5 × 17 cm each.

Fig.2 Vera (left) and François (right) Molnar dressed as Malevich for a masked ball, at their home in Paris, 198

other's thinking. We might say, then, that the two squares represent their two fields, science and art, and their interaction through abstract computer graphics.

Another interpretation, which I entertain here, is that this book tells another love story: that of the artist falling in love with the computer screen. *Love-Story (à l'ordinateur)* registers a pivotal moment in Molnar's career and in early computer graphics more generally that has been overlooked in histories of both art and technology: the advent of the computer screen and the shift that it signaled from so-called blind computing to interactive computing. To discuss this, I explore the material qualities of this artist's book—namely, the fact that it is made of what we might call early screenshots, snapshots or photographs that Molnar took of the computer screen.

By emphasizing these material traces of early computer graphics, I draw on methods from media archaeology.[2] While art history typically focuses on the final result of an artistic process and perhaps also on the preliminary sketches and studies, media archaeology focuses on processes, including those that are imperceptible to human sensory systems. In Molnar's case, a media-archaeological lens enables me to examine the experiential aspects of working with early computer graphics, such as the temporality of programming and creating visualizations as well as how human and nonhuman agents work in tandem.

Screenshots from the 1970s

Love-Story is materially different from most of Molnar's computational artworks, which are typically plotter drawings, executed in black ink on white paper by the robotic arm of a plotter. With *Love-Story,* she inverts this black-on-white paradigm, instead showing white squares on a black background [Fig. 3]. The white lines seem to glow, their edges soft and sometimes haloed, recalling Man Ray's *Space Writing*. Each page shows two squares in different configurations. The light appears more blurred or smeared in certain images, suggesting either the slight movement of the camera in the artist's hand or perhaps the rendering of the image on-screen happening faster than the camera's exposure time. The book consists of glossy photographs—screenshots—mounted on cardboard pages in an accordion fold, the first and last pages attached so that the book forms a loop.[3] It can be stood upright on a flat surface so that the glossiness of the paper has a reflective effect, like a dark computer screen. It can also be manipulated by hand, which lets the reader or viewer compare successive configurations of the squares.

A screenshot from the 1970s is a rare find. I use this term anachronistically; as architectural historian Matthew Allen explains, the word *screenshot,* derived from the word *snapshot,* an informal photograph, did not appear in print until 1983.[4] Unlike screenshots today, captured with the push of a button, early screenshots were taken with an external photographic camera pointed at the computer screen, which was usually a cathode-ray-tube (CRT) screen. As Allen points out, these photographs were often as ephemeral as the on-screen images they captured. The image known as the first screenshot was captured in 1959 by a young US Air Force officer, who snapped

Fig. 3

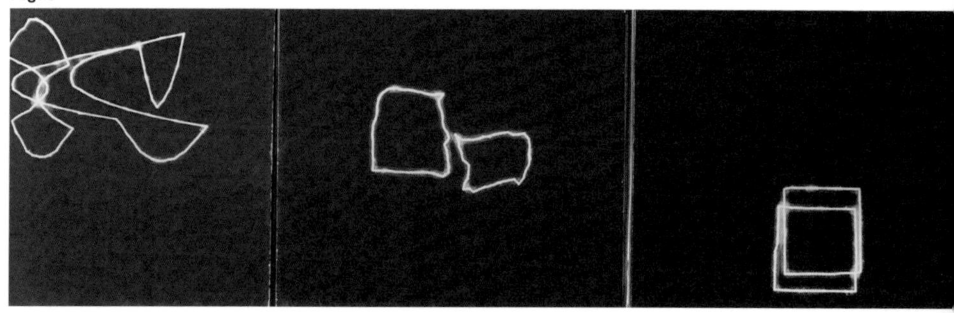

a Polaroid of the display console of the military computer, part of the US SAGE defense system. On this circular screen, we can make out the outline of a pinup girl, which was used to test the system. It was not until the 1960s that screenshots became valuable objects in computer-aided design and architecture. As Allen notes, designers developed a set of conventions for screenshots, such as the white-on-black aesthetic, to specifically differentiate these images from computer-aided drawings.[5] Ivan Sutherland, architect of the landmark early computer graphics program Sketchpad, wrote about his attempt to capture the "twinkle" of the CRT, to give the impression of a screen in the image.[6] The aim was to emphasize the screenness of these images to promote this new way of interacting with computers. Though Molnar was not involved in these early discourses on computer-aided design, her screenshots similarly capture a historic moment in the history of computer graphics—the advent of the screen—and the possibilities it offered for making art with computers.

Before the mid-1980s, the production of computer graphics remained limited to sites that housed mainframe computers, including military complexes, well-funded private corporations, and research laboratories such as the Centre Inter-Régional de Calcul Electronique (CIRCE), where Molnar was informally working.[7] Once personal computers became more ubiquitous, digital art could be consumed in its native environment—on the same machines on which it was produced. By contrast, early users of computer graphics relied on more traditional methods to preserve, document, and share their work beyond the computer lab: screen-based graphics had to be transposed to ink on paper. There was no way to "save" the image exactly as it appeared on the screen. Hard copies could be made using plotters or display copiers, neither of which was entirely faithful to the screen image, since both processes entailed flipping the light and dark values, like printing a photograph from a negative. The on-screen image was rather elusive—difficult to capture exactly as it appeared because of lighting conditions.

I want to suggest that, for Molnar, capturing screenshots had to do not only with the aesthetics of the image—the way the light lines contrasted with the dark surface of the screen—but also with the experience of using the CRT. Like snapshots, her screenshots convey an informality. These photographs document her fascination with what she calls the "fugitive" image, the ephemeral on-screen visualization that would soon disappear, but which indicated the way the screen would transform her process.[8]

From Blind to Interactive Computing

When Molnar first began experimenting with a mainframe computer in 1968, she could not see what she was doing. At that time, computing was a so-called blind process, meaning that programmers had to give instructions to the computer using the numbers on a punch card. They then had to wait hours—sometimes days—to see the results, which had to be output to paper using a plotter. This all changed when CIRCE purchased an IBM 2250 CRT display in the early 1970s.[9] A CRT screen was essentially the same hardware as a television set, minus the antennae for receiving signals. Along with other peripheral devices, such as a flatbed plotter, it could be hooked up to a mainframe computer—in Molnar's case, an IBM system/370—to display the results of a program within seconds. The first computer to use a CRT as a graphical output device was the Whirlwind, an American vacuum-tube computer, in late 1949. While CRTs became ubiquitous in American computer labs by the mid-1960s, there was often at least a two-year lag in bringing this kind of hardware to western Europe.[10]

In French, the CRT screen was called an *écran de visualisation*, and for Molnar it did just that—it took a program written in a programming language, in alphanumeric code, and visualized it, or made it visual. For Molnar, the most amazing thing about the CRT was its speed. Where a plotter took minutes or hours to output an image, the CRT did it in seconds. The IBM 2250 was a vector-display model, meaning its screen had electron guns that could draw lines between two points specified by the user. It could generate images of straight lines, points, and characters on a surface of about thirty-by-thirty centimeters.

What was so exciting about the CRT screen for Molnar? To understand its impact, we must first look at her journey with computers. In the early 1960s, before she had access to a computer lab, Molnar developed a methodology called the "machine imaginaire" that emulated a computer using step-by-step instructions and combinatorial mathematics to produce series of drawings.[11] This process hinged on two key actions: the comparison and the evaluation of successive images. Of course, she still had to execute these drawings by hand, which was time-consuming and inconsistent. Once Molnar began working with a *machine réelle*, the mainframe computer, she had not only more precise results but also more time to compare and evaluate images, since the computer greatly sped up her process. The CRT screen, with its "instantaneous" output, sped it up even more by reducing the wait time between giving instructions and receiving results, delivering them in glowing green lines right before her eyes in a matter of seconds. As a result, the CRT enabled Molnar to conduct controlled, systematic experiments about her own artistic subjectivity, examining the ways in which she made aesthetic decisions using her intuitive reasoning. The idea was not to generate a preconceived, preprogrammed composition but rather to investigate the process of composition.

Molnar called this method of working "conversational," her neologism for a controlled mode of working with a mainframe computer connected to two terminals: the CRT screen and a plotter. The conversational method is first mentioned in her article for the journal *Leonardo*, penned in 1974 and published the following year.[12] *Conversational* was likely an imperfect English translation of *conversationnel*, the French term for interactivity in computing. While more recent notions of interactive computing refer to a virtual environment where one can manipulate virtual objects, this earlier definition of interactivity refers to "real-time, two-way exchanges across the interface [or the computer screen] between user and machine."[13]

Molnar's conversational method worked as follows: She would run her program on the mainframe, view the results on the CRT screen, and then compare and evaluate successive variations, making changes to her parameters as she went along. When an image pleased her, she would output it to paper. Once she had a series of plotter drawings, she would lay them on the floor and make further comparisons, deciding on a sequence to show the images and occasionally going back to the computer to make more, repeating parts of the process. Unlike many "systematic" artists of her generation, Molnar's process had no distinct beginning, middle, or end; it was more of a shuttling back and forth, a series of translations from code to image, from screen to page and back again.

Tool or Collaborator?

Early user-machine interactivity was often described using a metaphor of conversation or dialogue. IBM's promotional material for the 2250 CRT display introduced the screen as an interlocutor that could bring "man and computer into a more active partnership."[14] The screen was conceptualized as a facilitator of human-computer communication, a very early instance of the graphical user interface (or GUI), with which all computer users are familiar today. The advent of interactivity raised an important question, which remains relevant: Is the computer a tool for artists, like a paintbrush or a camera obscura? Or is it a collaborator?

Often, such metaphors gave agency to these inanimate machines. A manual of interactive computer graphics published in 1976 presented the CRT screen as an "ideal tool" for approaching the "symbiosis between Man and machine," suggesting that this partnership could produce results beyond anything that either human or machine intelligence could achieve on its own.[15] In other words, because interactive computing was modeled on dialogue or conversation, the computer was, in turn, often referred to as a design partner or collaborator. The interface gave the computer a face and even a mind of its own. Molnar's writing from this period demonstrates resistance to this new understanding of computing. Although her husband's bookshelf was filled with books on artificial intelligence, she distanced herself from the idea. And whereas fellow computer art pioneer Manfred Mohr referred to the computer as his "partner," Molnar insisted the computer was merely a tool.[16] She kept the term "conversational" in scare quotes, suggesting that she was never *really* talking to the computer. If the computer were a person, Molnar would dryly joke, it would be subhuman, a "slave" that would do whatever she wanted without complaint.[17]

Molnar's screenshots, however, seem to tell a different story. There is an intimacy or a softness to these images that is missing from the artist's plotter drawings. And there is also a sentimentality. While Molnar's screenshots rarely appear in her oeuvre, she held onto them over the years, tucking them away in her archive alongside snapshots of family and friends. Recalling her first encounter with the CRT screen, she lights up, describing a feeling of "rebirth" akin to when she first set foot in Paris in 1947.[18] This suggests that Molnar embraced interactive computing more than she let on.

Embracing the interactive possibilities of the early computer screen moved Molnar's work in a different direction from that of her peers, both her fellow pioneers in digital art and other painters, who were using systems and seriality to investigate artistic subjectivity. She used the screen to develop a method of working iteratively that led to new insight into her creative process. For Molnar, the computer is not humanoid. Rather, it brings us closer to understanding human creativity. If she saw the mainframe computer itself as merely a tool, its peripheral devices—namely, the CRT display—took on a different role, the more active role of interlocutor. Molnar could not complete her pictorial experiments nor her series of images without having these on-screen visualizations to respond to. If working with the mainframe was like notating choreography, working with the computer screen was like performing a pas de deux.

Molnar's screenshots complicate a question that is often asked of early digital art: Is the art the code or the drawing? These images draw our attention to what happens in between, emphasizing the temporal processes of early computing and computer graphics. They highlight the experimental nature of this art form, which was evolving along with developments in the technologies that it employed. The screenshots help us to think beyond this linear model of input and output that is so often attributed to computer-generated art, especially when it is compared to conceptual art à la Sol LeWitt: a set of instructions that could be carried out by anyone or anything.[19] Molnar's playful process indicates that artists were not necessarily detached from the *déroulement* (or unfolding) of their programs. They could be actively involved in the process of executing a program, even modifying it as it went along.

The accordion fold of *Love-Story* suggests that there is no clear linear narrative to this story—no discrete beginning, middle, or end. The viewer must manipulate the folds, going back and forth between images and comparing different variations, just as Molnar did on the computer screen. By introducing spatiality with the accordion fold, Molnar also introduces a process of interaction, creating a dialogue between the reader/viewer and the book/object that mimics that of the artist and the computer screen. In other words, although the book is a physical object, it maintains characteristics of Molnar's nonlinear computational process.

Vera Molnar's screenshots highlight the interconnectedness of the histories of art, technology, and media and the possibilities of using interdisciplinary methodologies to bring nuance to art historical investigations of new media art. By tracing the material history of early computer graphics—and going beyond what the artist has made (publicly) visible—we might find more objects like these, which bear witness to historical moments of collaboration, cooperation, or simply conversation between humans and machines. //

[1] Turning the images into a book might also be read as an art historical reference to El Lissitzky's constructivist artist's book *About Two Squares* (1922). It also recalls Norton Juster's *The Dot and the Line: A Romance in Lower Mathematics* (1963), a picture book about a dot hopelessly in love with a line. Molnar's title, however, was a tongue-in-cheek reference to the pulp novel by the American author Erich Segal, which was all the rage in Paris after its French translation was published in 1971. Vera Molnar, conversation with the author, November 14, 2020.

[2] Wolfgang Ernst, "Media Archaeography: Method and Machine versus History and Narrative of Media," in *Media Archaeology:*

Approaches, Applications, and Implications, ed. Erkki Huhtamo and Jussi Parikka (Berkeley: University of California Press, 2011), 239–55.

[3] While the location of the original accordion-fold book is unknown, there is an extant maquette in the Szöllősi-Nagy—Nemes Collection, in Hungary [Fig. 3]. This maquette is only a partial accordion, which does not connect at the ends.

[4] Matthew Allen, "Representing Computer-Aided Design: Screenshots and the Interactive Computer circa 1960," *Perspectives on Science* 24, no. 6 (2016): 637–68.

[5] Allen, "Representing Computer-Aided Design," 637–68.

[6] Quoted in Allen, "Representing Computer-Aided Design," 657. The original source is a 1963 dissertation by Ivan Sutherland, titled "Sketchpad, A Man-Machine Graphical Communication System."

[7] Molnar was under the impression that she was the only user at CIRCE interested in the CRT screen. Vera Molnar, conversation with the author, August 30, 2017.

[8] Molnar was not the first nor the only artist to point her camera at a computer screen; see Herbert W. Franke's "oscillographs," Ben Laposky's "oscillons," and Mary Ellen Bute's experimental animations. While these computer graphics were analog rather than digital, these artists also used photography to capture ephemeral images that were difficult to document otherwise.

[9] While it is not entirely clear when CIRCE purchased the IBM 2250, an October 1972 report is the first to mention "l'unité de visualisation" that is labeled "2250." See CIRCE, "Rapport au Comité de Direction du CIRCE," October 20, 1972, Archives Nationales de France, 20140644/131: 3, dossiers des laboratoires du Centre National de la Recherche Scientifique (CNRS). The earliest extant "screenshot" in Molnar's studio is from

1973, the same year she first mentioned the *écran cathodique* in her 1973 lecture "L'œil qui pense," written for the SIGMA festival in Bordeaux. The lecture notes are held at Molnar's archives in Paris.

[10] Richard A. Guedj, "The Challenge of Computer Graphics in Continental Western Europe," *Proceedings of the IEEE* 62, no. 4 (1974): 421.

[11] Molnar borrowed this terminology from her friend Michel Philippot, a composer who made music with instructions.

[12] Vera Molnar, "Toward Aesthetic Guidelines for Paintings with the Aid of a Computer," *Leonardo* 8, no. 3 (1975): 185–89.

[13] Thierry Bardini, *Bootstrapping: Douglas Engelbart, Coevolution, and the Origins of Personal Computing* (Stanford, CA: Stanford University Press, 2000), 19.

[14] IBM and Pacific Productions, *Frontiers in Computer Graphics*, 1967.

[15] Pierre Morvan and Michel Lucas, *Images et ordinateur. Introduction à l'infographie interactive* (Paris: Larousse, 1976), 11. See also Joseph C. R. Licklider, "Man-Computer Symbiosis," *IRE Transactions on Human Factors in Electronics* 1 (March 1960): 4–11.

[16] Jean-François Bory, ed., *L'Humidité*, no. 5 (1971).

[17] See *Un peintre et son robot*, directed by Fabienne Wiazemski, 1981. Until recently, computing discourse made frequent use of the slave/master metaphor, language that the computing community is still in the process of rewriting.

[18] Molnar, conversation with the author, August 30, 2017.

[19] Victoria Salinger points out that this comparison offers a reductive understanding of not only early computer art but also conceptual art. Victoria Salinger, "'Writing Calculations, Calculating Writing': Hanne Darboven's Computer Art," *Grey Room*, no. 65 (Fall 2016): 37.

#02

CATHODIC ART IN FRANCE: FROM EXPERIMENTING WITH THE MEDIUM TO EXPERIENCING THE MEDIA

Fleur Chevalier

Writing in 2003, artist David Robbins, whose work is infused with the question of the relationship between art and mass entertainment, commented on the work of his colleague Pierre Huyghe: "Take digital video cameras. Anyone who holds one of these cameras is no longer obliged to think only of video art, of the old ghetto place of video art; camera in hand, these people can now think 'television' or 'film' without deluding themselves with vain hopes."[1] It is difficult to fully understand the significance of this phrase and the semantic contradictions it raises without knowing the history of artists who have actually attempted to work in the context of television. What does Robbins mean by "old ghetto place of video art"? What does it mean to "think 'television' or 'film'"? What "vain hopes" is he talking about?

Although there are collections of video art in museums, video art is absent from the French mainstream TV industry, where the technological format matters little compared to the media format of a program calibrated for commercialization. Television programmers barely care whether the product they buy was recorded on 35 or 16 mm film or on one-half-inch or three-quarter-inch tape. What matters most is the type of program, which will determine the broadcasting slot: drama, documentary, talk show, commercial, music video, newscast, et cetera. Thus, when Robbins invites us to think about film or television, he is not thinking about the film as an object or about the materiality of the cathodic image; he is referring to the production standards of commercial cinema and television. The artists who have tried to work with television have not always reasoned in these terms.

Since the 1960s, artists animated by "vain hopes" have taken advantage of access to sophisticated equipment within television studios to explore the aesthetic potential of electronic images and to conduct their own visual research. As the argument of demiurgic inspiration does not prevail over the commercial imperatives governing the media industry, these creators have had to adapt to the economic mutations of the audiovisual industry. In France, this transformation mainly took place between 1974 and 1987, from the dismantling of the Office de radiodiffusion-télévision française (ORTF) to the partial privatization of the television broadcasting networks. We need only observe the careers of the artists involved in this story to understand how, progressively, television has imposed a battery of hegemonic codes on contemporary visual artists. For the artists who work in the field of television, specific questions arise: How to find a place in a structure dedicated to the distribution of formatted products? How to infiltrate the gaps in an industry hostile to any optical deviation? As soon as these problems are raised, different concepts of video art are strengthened and, confronted with the rigidity of the standards imposed by TV, the desire to explore the electronic image is replaced by that of subverting the media rhetoric and space.

Robert Cahen and Matthieu Laurette: Two Cathodic Artists

Let us study the cases of Robert Cahen and Matthieu Laurette, both represented in the video-art collection of the Centre Pompidou. These artists have radically different positions as regards images, yet both have worked in the context of French television.

As a pioneer of electronic images, Cahen joined the ORTF's research department in 1969, when he was part of the internship of the Groupe de Recherches Musicales (GRM), directed by the composer Pierre Schaeffer. In 1973, as part of the Groupe de Recherche Image (GRI), also attached to the research department, Cahen produced his first tape, titled *L'Invitation au voyage*.[2] Working in the ORTF studios gave the video artist the opportunity to use the Truqueur Universel, developed in 1968 by engineer Francis Coupigny. This synthesizer makes it possible to colorize images, solarize them, overprint several images, and generate geometric forms, resulting in new images, with stunning plasticity.

In 1974, the dismantling of the ORTF led to the disappearance of the GRI. The Institut National de l'Audiovisuel (INA) was created at the last minute to take over, particularly in terms of research and the conservation of archives. The GRI was reborn in 1979 under the impetus of a partnership with the Ecole Nationale Supérieure des Arts Décoratifs (ENSAD), which had just been equipped with a brand-new video studio. This opening benefited several French video artists. There, Thierry Kuntzel developed a body of work that is now famous but rarely studied in relation to the standards of the TV industry. Criticism of photographic realism, however, forms the core of Kuntzel's first electronic experiments. Throughout his writings, the artist willingly opposed the pictorial nature of his images to the illusionism promoted by the industry: "With the exception of a few rare films [...] cinema was reduced to a pornographic album, the light forgotten for the frame, the scene, the displaying of objects—for the butcher's stall, the display: industry, commerce."[3]

Other creators passed through GRI to produce experimental tapes, such as Catherine Ikam, Geneviève Hervé, Marc'O, Colette Deblé, Claude Torey, and Patrick Prado. Although produced in the context of television, these videos are rarely aired. Moreover, access to equipment for video artists who could not be accommodated in the INA studios was a real problem, unless they were students at ENSAD or could take advantage of the video studio at the Centre Pompidou, which was opened to a few artists invited by the museum in 1978. At the beginning of the 1980s, several local cultural institutions acquired equipment. In Paris, the association Vidéo Ciné Troc hosted a few video artists after acquiring a one-half-inch unit in 1978. Founded in 1982, the Grand Canal collective began distributing videos produced on the fringe of the mainstream networks before acquiring, albeit belatedly, a U-Matic three-quarter-inch editing bench in 1987. In order to have access to more efficient machines, many people worked in postproduction houses at night or on weekends, outside the working hours of professional technicians, but this was not a sustainable strategy.

Matthieu Laurette, a contemporary artist trained on the art-school circuit, moved into a completely different field when he chose to turn to television in 1994. He recorded a commercial for the program *Rapido Annonces*, broadcast on the cable music channel MCM: "Hi, my name is Matthieu, I'm an artist, and I offer to feed you for free," Laurette said on air, inviting viewers to contact him for more information. The artist had indeed found it possible to live for free by buying only products subject to appealing offers such as "100 percent refund" or "cash back." Laurette generously proposed to share this epiphany with consumers through traveling showrooms, supermarket visits, and television appearances.

In 1997, an article published on the front page of *Le Monde* helped Laurette advance to a new level in terms of media coverage: he gained access to the France 2 television news.[4] During each of his television appearances, when his status as an artist was mentioned, it was only to specify that Laurette was on social welfare benefits, which led him to hone this clever tactic. Twisting the cliché of the miserable and tormented genius à la Van Gogh, Laurette presented himself as an average consumer, devoid of excess and charisma, displaying a blissful confidence in the opportunities offered to him among the supermarket aisles. Laurette's speech appears calibrated for television: attractive, simple, and repetitive—"between the banal and the original." I deliberately use the words of structuralist theorist Abraham Moles when he defines "artistic work" as "a message that, if it is to be apprehended by the average individual, a member of the public, must be understood in a certain range between the banal and the original, measured by its redundancy."[5]

Laurette negotiated this turn toward television while he was still a student at the Ecole Supérieure d'Art de Grenoble. He practiced videography without being satisfied with the means at his disposal, the results, or the broadcasting and viewing conditions of his work. On the other hand, in his view, "television combines this possibility of having an audience, a means of production, a place for broadcasting."[6] Still, according to the artist, nobody can escape the entertainment society: "And therefore, if we must participate in it, we might as well have the same tools and be able to make choices."[7] This is how Laurette decided to integrate into the television scene as it currently functions. Thus, the work of Laurette seems to echo the practical observations of Andy Warhol: "Video art? There is no video art, we're trying to be commercial … Have you watched video art on TV and seen how awful it is? Commercial TV is the best."[8]

In the United States—in spite of the Public Broadcasting Service network's favoring the emergence of experimental laboratories, or TV Labs, hosted by local channels such as KQED (San Francisco), WGBH (Boston), and WNET 13 (New York)—television was and remains commercial, unlike in France, where it began as a state-run body.[9] However, the dismantling of the ORTF in 1974 was the first step in a shift by the French TV industry toward a more liberal setup. One initially positive consequence can be observed in the field of television design. In 1975, graphic identity became an issue because of the new competition between channels, which had become TV program companies. The channel Antenne 2 tried to distinguish itself from TF1 and FR3 with a logo drawn by the painter Georges Mathieu and a psychedelic electronic clock designed by Peter Foldès, a pioneer from GRI.

A second stage was reached in 1984, with the launch of the private subscription channel Canal+, and then, in 1986, two new channels went on air: La Cinq and TV6, replaced by M6 in 1987. Directed by CEOs Jérôme Seydoux, Jean Riboud, and Silvio Berlusconi, La Cinq pursued a purely commercial policy. The INA gradually withdrew from experimental production, a trend made worse by the privatization of TF1 in 1987. Competition, while initially stimulating, became a pretext for leveling out the TV industry: all the channels aligned themselves to offer the same products.

Matthieu Laurette's career must be viewed in this context and measured against that of other artists, such as Robert Cahen, who see images above all as a *plastic* horizon to be explored. For Laurette, the image seems to be a space to be subverted and television a supermarket—a distribution network, strictly speaking. Although their concepts of images are opposed, the works of Laurette and Cahen answer each other through the history of French television.

The Advent of Diversionary Practices

In the 1980s, cathodic works that were less about video experimentation than about media subversion came to the fore. At the crossroads of the experimental sector and post-situationism, Kiki Picasso is a good illustration of this phenomenon. In 1984, this former member of the graphic punk collective Bazooka became passionate about graphic palettes. By chance, Antenne 2 opened its doors to him in 1986, when two producers asked him to make teasers for a variety program called *C'est encore mieux l'après-midi* (1985–87). The idea was to produce one "provocative" jingle per week in the same pop and aggressive vein that had contributed to the graphic success of Bazooka in the newspaper *Libération* (1977–78). Kiki Picasso performed by subverting images that he graffitied and reprocessed using the channel's Paint Box in a firecracker visual style, full of references to the Russian avant-garde or pop art. This taste for pastiche ironically emphasized the satirical scope of these teasers, especially since, during this period, the video artist did not hesitate to plunder the raw documents recorded by journalists, stored in the hallways of Antenne 2.

Unable to satisfy his fantasy of appearing on television news, Kiki Picasso devised several clips, commercials, and designs, before founding his own production company, Art Force Industrie, in 1988.[10] His mission was to prove that on television, "art is simply viable [and that] there is no reason to always make soup, to always be neutral."[11] Thanks to the financial support of producer Michèle Gavras, the studio was equipped with state-of-the-art technology, enabling Kiki Picasso to design a summer program broadcast in the afternoon on FR3, *40° à l'ombre de la 3*. Although sponsorship from Philips also helped him to show Art Force Industrie productions as part of this same program, the artist did not succeed in finding support from the channels to launch an audiovisual creation program.

Following the partial privatization of the French television network, the 1990s were marked by a restoration of order in the field of TV. Visual audacity was banned, and to survive, independent video artists turned to making documentaries. In view of this shutdown, televisual subversion finally won out as the best way to remain visible in an economy where experimental production appeared not only expensive but also useless, justifying its ghettoization.

In 1991, as a tangible sign of this shift, Canal+ launched a new televisual creation program called *L'Œil du cyclone*, directed by Alain Burosse, Pascale Faure, and Patrice Bauchy. Each week, the program was structured around a specific theme and took the form of an often-humorous montage. The principle evoked that of the cinematographic subversion promoted by Guy Debord. Devoted to situationism, the sixteenth episode of *L'Œil du cyclone* convinced Debord to work on a final televisual subversion, *Guy Debord, son art et son temps*, an alarming montage of archives in the guise of a televisual testament, produced by Canal+ in 1994.[12]

The Image as a Territory: From the Agora to the Supermarket

For devotees of misappropriation, images are both a treasure to be subverted and a ready-made object to be recycled. Their misappropriation enables the subversion of the values they convey. But hijacking also implies territory to conquer. If television is a device, isn't the image a gateway enabling us to occupy the televisual space?[13]

Well before the 1990s, the concept of the image as a place was developed and explored by telecommunication artists Kit

Galloway and Sherrie Rabinowitz.[14] The idea also motivated the participative television experiments led in the United States by such artists as Allan Kaprow, Douglas Davis, or Stan VanDerBeek, who saw in the cathodic image an agora to be opened up to viewers. The most representative artist of this trend in France was undoubtedly Fred Forest, for whom video practice was entirely subordinate to his mission as a "sociological" artist: "video art doesn't exist—*video is not an artistic instrument: it is an intersubjective epistemological tool.*"[15]

His most famous work, *Space Media*, illustrates this attitude. Launched in 1972, the operation, carried out several times, involved simultaneously occupying the press and television to let the public speak. In the first version, Forest initially bought an advertisement in the pages of *Le Monde des arts*. Deliberately leaving this media space blank, he asked readers to claim it as they wished before returning the result to him. In the same vein, a few days later, the artist organized the broadcasting of a "blank minute" during the program *Télé Midi* on channel one.[16] During this symbolic minute, Forest urged the public to use the time for independent thought. Targeted at the emancipation of the masses, the approach is in line with the continuation of the debates of May 1968. The artist reinterprets the collaborative slogan from a poster such as *L'Etat c'est chacun de nous* (The state is each of us), which invites the viewer to reconsider the blank space as outlined by the contours of an isolated character awaiting the help of their peers to write the future.

Thus, for Forest, before being a medium, an image is a place where we establish relations with our fellow citizens. Consequently, when the artist asserted that "this tool [the video] renews our vision of reality," he thought not of going beyond the visual norms promoted by the mainstream industry but rather of opening the eyes of the spectator to the realities of contemporary society.[17] Is this not also the case with Matthieu Laurette?

He employed images as a forum, uniting viewers around a popular fantasy: free consumption. In a society where advertising suggests that emancipation comes through consumption, Laurette suggested freeing oneself by taking advantage of the absurdities of marketing. Being pragmatic, the artist traded the dream of establishing horizontal communication for the purpose of working to subvert the system, without appearing to do so, by exploiting its flaws. In the mid-1990s, by presenting himself to the public as a standard consumer rather than as a liberating hero, Laurette responded with irony to the ideals of May 1968, in light of the evolution of the media landscape.

Indeed, in 1998, to celebrate the thirtieth anniversary of the popular uprising, Laurette submitted a caustic reading of the situationist project through a piece entitled *Le spectacle n'est pas terminé*.[18] In May 1998, the Spectacle channel, a concession of the CanalSatellite package, planned to produce a program to celebrate the anniversary of May 1968. Laurette was invited and asked to shoot his contribution to the program on the Champs-Elysées, where he called out to passersby to suggest that they read some excerpts from *La Société du spectacle*. These selected excerpts were written on a white board so that they could be read in front of the camera, like on a teleprompter. Recited in this way in a mecca of Parisian consumerism and on the microphone of such a channel, Guy Debord's critical remarks became advertising slogans. The anniversary became a commemoration. The result had all the makings of a masquerade of ideological emancipation. What about the artist as a redeeming messiah? On television, no one escapes the coercive economy of the show, not even Debord, whose theses are soluble in the televisual industry.

Thus, Matthieu Laurette's works benefit from being put in perspective with those of a sociological performer such as Fred Forest or an experimental video artist such as Robert Cahen.

Although their works are all classified as video art, the artists' approaches are never actually compared to each other. With reason, objects produced in the orbit of television are often analyzed without consideration of the environment and history that bring them together. This history is not only that of fine arts but also that of television. Artists who work directly with television are interested in what is specific to it—namely, the cathodic image. This formula refers to a medium—the electronic image—and to the media environment so as to embrace the variety of audiovisual practices developed in the orbit of television. The cathodic image is simultaneously a medium, a consumer product, a fragment of media rhetoric, and a fortress to occupy. For almost all experimental video artists, the very possibility of being able to carry out plastic experiments on electronic images is directly correlated to that of being able to oppose an alternative discourse within the media, as shown by Kiki Picasso's company. However, the economics of television have dealt a fatal blow to this branch of televisual creation, confirming David Robbins's view that experimental video artists' research is now futile. Still, the stance of these marginalized artists goes well beyond our consumerist relationship with images by proposing not only to misappropriate the products of mass television distribution but also to subvert the visual norms that format our very perception of the world. //

[1] David Robbins, "Science-fiction chaude," in *Pierre Huyghe. Le Château de Turing* (Dijon: Les presses du réel, 2003), 172. Translation by Natasha Pittet, Scribe Ltd.

[2] Robert Cahen, *L'Invitation au voyage* (France, 1973), produced by ORTF, 2-inch video, 9:00, color, sound.

[3] Thierry Kuntzel, "Notes du 23 février 1979," in *Title TK, Notes 1974–1992*, ed. Anne-Marie Duguet (Nantes and Paris: Musée des Beaux-Arts; Anarchive, 2006), 167. Translation by Natasha Pittet, Scribe Ltd.

[4] See Pascale Kremer, "Demain, on mange gratis," *Le Monde*, May 16, 1997, front page; newscast broadcast on May 16, 1997, 1:00 and 8:38 p.m.

5 Abraham Moles, *Art et ordinateur* (Paris: Casterman, 1971), 21. Translation by Natasha Pittet, Scribe Ltd.

6 Quoted in Pierre-Charles T.-Monahan, "L'Insolite Spectaculaire. Entretien avec Matthieu Laurette," *ETC*, no. 96 (June–October 2012): 45. Translation by Natasha Pittet, Scribe Ltd.

7 T.-Monahan, "L'Insolite Spectactulaire," 46.

8 Quoted in Lynn Spigel, "Warhol's Everyday TV," in "Art TV Clash," special issue, *Multitudes* 2, no. 5 (May 2010): 165.

9 KQED opened a laboratory in 1967 with funding from the Rockefeller Foundation and a grant from the National Endowment for the Arts (NEA). WGBH opened an experimental lab the same year with Rockefeller Foundation support. In 1971, WNET's TV Lab was supported by the Rockefeller Foundation, the NEA, and the New York State Council on the Arts.

10 See, e.g., the clip for *L'Arrivée du tour* (1986) by Alain Bashung or the credits for the program *Télé Caroline* (1988) aired on FR3.

11 Quoted in Thierry Defert and Jean-Baptiste Touchard, "Kiki Picasso. Art Force Industrie. 'Liberté totale, l'Art est viable …,'" *Pixel. Le magazine des nouvelles images*, no. 2 (November–December 1988): 53. Translation by Natasha Pittet, Scribe Ltd.

12 See *Cette situation doit changer* (France, 1992), directed by Bertrand Mérino-Péris and Brigitte Cornand, produced by Canal+, first broadcast April 4, 1992, video, 28:00, color, sound; and *Guy Debord, son art et son temps* (France, 1994), written by Guy Debord, directed by Brigitte Cornand, produced by Canal+ and INA, first broadcast January 9, 1995, TV movie, 60:00, black and white, sound.

13 I use "device" as defined by Michel Foucault and synthesized by Giorgio Agamben; see Agamben, *Qu'est-ce qu'un dispositif?* (Paris: Rivages, 2014), 31.

14 See "Defining the Image as Place. A Conversation with Kit Galloway, Sherrie Rabinowitz and Gene Youngblood," *High Performance*, no. 37 (1987): 52–59.

15 Fred Forest, *Art sociologique, vidéo* (Paris: Union Générale d'Edition, 1977), 67. Italics in the original. Translation by Natasha Pittet, Scribe Ltd.

16 *Space Media, Télé Midi*, produced for channel one, first broadcast January 20, 1972.

17 Forest, *Art sociologique*, 67.

18 *Le spectacle n'est pas terminé*, 1998, video, 2:30, color, sound; from the collection of the Centre National des Arts Plastiques.

Videography and Archives

Alain Burosse, Pascale Faure, and Patrice Bauchy, dir., *L'Œil du cyclone*, 1991–99, broadcast on Canal+; available at https://vimeo.com/channels/231310/.

Robert Cahen, online videos, http://robertcahen.com.

Matthieu Laurette, *Free Sample Demix*, anthology edited by the Jousse Gallery in 1998, www.laurette.net/data/download/pdf/ML_freesampledemix_1998.pdf.

Matthieu Laurette, *Matthieu Laurette: Selected Works (1993–2003)*, www.laurette.net/data/download/pdf/dossier_laurette_hi.pdf.

Kiki Picasso, credits of the program *Télé Caroline*, 1988, broadcast on FR3; available at www.ina.fr/video/I09019264/generique-de-tele-caroline-video.html.

Kiki Picasso, *L'Arrivée du tour*, produced by Riff/Barclay, video clip for Alain Bashung, 1986, 4:00, color, sound; available at www.youtube.com/watch?v=tbysVvk5AFE/.

Studio of the Ecole des Beaux-Arts, Paris, *L'Etat c'est chacun de nous*, May 1968, poster, http://gallica.bnf.fr/ark:/12148/btv1b90180462?rk=42918;4/.

03

LIVE ON TWITCH: THE ART HISTORY CLASSIFICATION OF PERFORMANCES IN DIGITAL GAMES

Katharina Brandl

> To be a performance artist, you have to hate theatre … Theatre is
> fake. The knife is not real, the blood is not real, and the emotions
> are not real. Performance is just the opposite: the knife is real,
> the blood is real, and the emotions are real.
> (Marina Abramović, 2010)

With statements such as these, Marina Abramović, a performance artist who is as celebrated as she is heavily criticized, summed up a certain preunderstanding of performance as a medium of the visual arts:[1] the authentic body, which, as in her well-known performance *Lips of Thomas* (1975), actually bleeds in the flesh and remains present even in a state of unconsciousness, also defined the spectacle of her retrospective and show at New York's Museum of Modern Art (MoMA) in 2010.[2] *The Artist Is Present* was the title not only of the exhibition but also of a feature-length documentary film about the project, which was released in cinemas internationally. Thus, the Marina Abramović phenomenon took the spectacle of the authentic self in exhibition spaces to the extreme.

Artistic performances in digital, streamed games do not accomplish anything of the sort, however. The "ketchup" is not real blood from a real body but merely from images of bodies. Avatars interact with one another and with the possibilities of game mechanics; sometimes, the performative action is no longer even mediated by the representation of avatars but merely by the effects enabled by artistic interventions in game worlds.[3] These effects result from the interaction of different human and nonhuman players, from software architectures, from commercial cloud server farms, and from economic interests. The ability of the performers to act is limited—not by individual, physical boundaries and institutional constraints of stage or exhibition spaces but by the mechanics of the game, the algorithms, and the software architecture.

This contrasts with the self-perception of artists that performances in digital games that can be streamed live—both in multiplayer environments and on platforms such as Twitch—are to be understood as such. When can we speak conclusively about performance as a medium in this type of work?

This article addresses the question of whether it is possible to develop a perspective based on the history and theory of performance as a medium of the visual arts that conclusively allows for the inclusion of these recent artistic phenomena. Whatever the outcome, this requires a theoretical recalibration, for which I propose two approaches here.

Let us start by focusing on the problem exemplified by Erika Fischer-Lichte's *Ästhetik des Performativen*.[4] This monograph, published in 2004, has enjoyed an impressive response, suggesting that it is the most influential reappraisal and theorization of artistic performance in the German-speaking world. Fischer-Lichte's definitions of an aesthetics of the performative clarify the challenge of talking about performances in digital, streamed games as such. Building on J. L. Austin's speech act theory, Fischer-Lichte describes performances as (a) constituting reality, (b) self-referential, and (c) dependent on social or institutional context. Although speech act theory as a theory of linguistic utterances cannot cover the current breadth of performative artistic practices, Austin's concept lives on in at least two descriptions of performances as a medium of the visual arts: in talk about the authentic body and about the ephemeral, the fleeting moment of action in the here and now, which has been emphasized not only in Fischer-Lichte's theory but also, for example, by writers such as Peggy Phelan in a US context.[5] Fischer-Lichte extends her conceptual approach by using another classic work in the theory of the performative, Judith Butler's essay "Performative Acts and Gender Constitution," concerning the aspect of (d) corporeality and, with reference to Max Hermann, that of (e) performance experience.[6] Fischer-Lichte's references to Austin and Butler ground her reflections on the properties of the performative in linguistics and cultural studies. The reference to Max Hermann, a central figure of German theater studies in the first decades of the twentieth century, on the other hand, directs our focus to the prioritization of the performance experience itself, which is also crucial for Fischer-Lichte.

Not all five cornerstones of Fischer-Lichte's theoretical network (constitution of reality, self-referentiality, context/institutionality, corporeality, and performance experience) apply to the same extent to performances in digital games. Her focus on the "corporeal copresence [...] of co-subjects" is obstructive to devising a concept for performances in streamed games.[7] Regardless of the institutional context of the work—that is, whether a performance takes place on the stage of a theater or in the exhibition spaces of visual art institutions—it is the corporeal copresence of all those present that constitutes the performance experience. The crux of the matter, then, lies in the nexus of the simultaneity of corporeal production and corporeal reception. But these two factors can also coincide in performances in digital games—for example, when Cao Fei holds a mayoral election in her fictitious city RMB City in the virtual world of *Second Life*, which is transmitted to the Serpentine

Gallery and simultaneously observed by other users on the platform itself.[8] Another example is the artist Angela Washko, who in her work *The Council on Gender Sensitivity and Behavioral Awareness in World of Warcraft* (2012–16), moves through the worlds of *World of Warcraft* and interacts with others present in the multiplayer environment. But the corporeal, authentic selves of the performers are quite evidently no longer the focus in either example.

Contemporary Forms of Liveness

Joseph DeLappe, whose artistic practice has involved digital games for two decades, described his work *Elegy: GTA USA Gun Homicides* (2018–19) [Figs. 1, 2] as both a performance and a mod, or modification, of the game *Grand Theft Auto V* (Rockstar North). In this work, only an algorithm performs—a previously defined set of rules, which has little to do with corporeality. For the work, DeLappe adapted the gangster blockbuster *Grand Theft Auto V*

Fig. 1

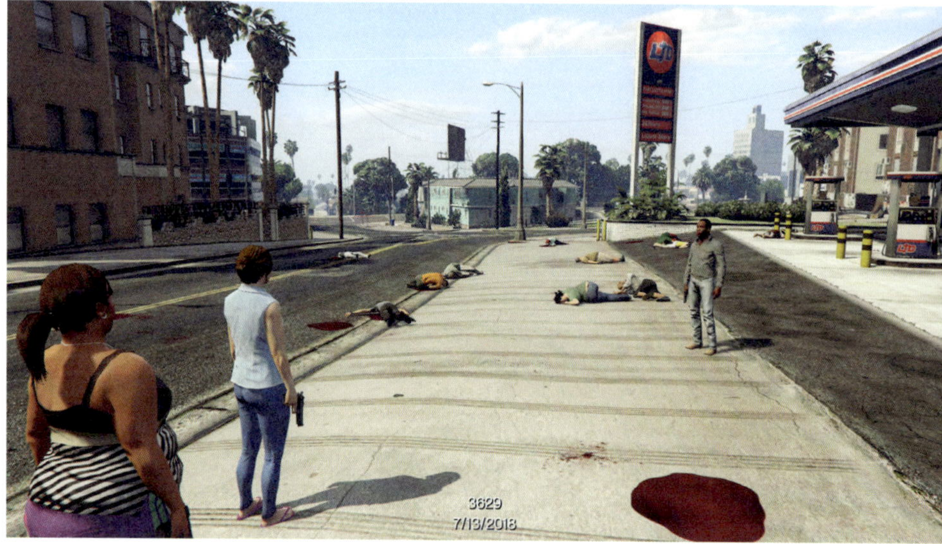

such that an avatar roamed through the game world throughout the day and displayed the number of gun murders (actually committed in the United States) every day since the beginning of the year. The daily murder statistics figure was automatically re-created in a twenty-four-hour stream on the Twitch platform. The stream was accessible from July 4, 2018, to July 4, 2019. The number of homicides by firearm re-created in the work on July 4, 2018, matched the total number of homicides committed since January 1 of the same year. By the end of the year, the number of homicides per day was added.[9] As time progressed, the images of homicides by firearms became more and more brutal, simply because there were more and more of them. On January 1, 2019, the statistics performance went back to zero.

The simultaneity of production and reception reflects the systemic locus that is crucial for performances: the connection between execution and performance. Specifically, the murder is both committed in real space and performed in digital space.

Figs. 1, 2 Joseph DeLappe, *Elegy: GTA USA Gun Homicides*, 2018–19, performance and modification of *Grand Theft Auto V* (Rockstar North).

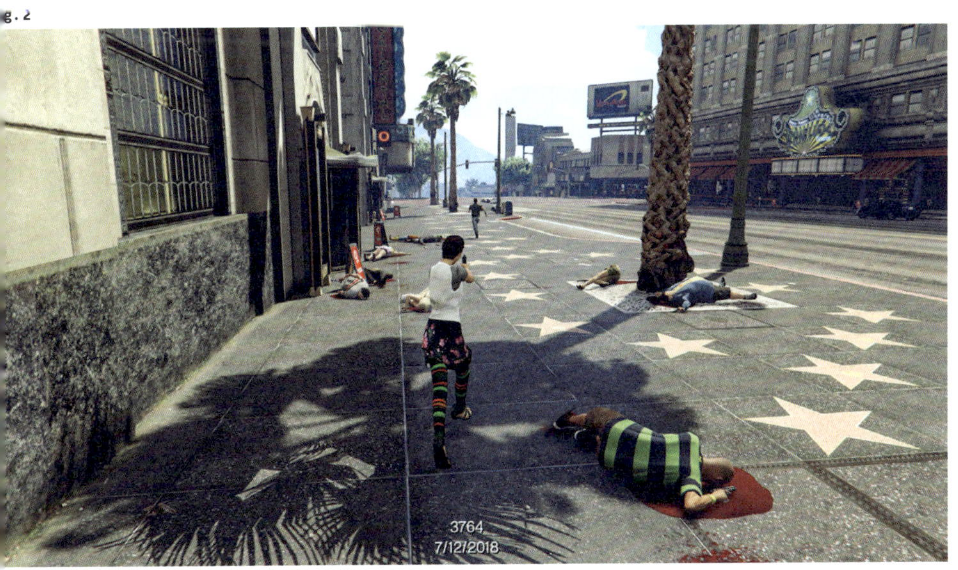

Through the theoretical emphasis on the copresence of viewers and performers in their respective corporealities, the sharing of space and time, which seems to characterize performances, is narrowed to an emphasis on a specific live situation, understood as authentic. Philip Auslander, in his widely acclaimed *Liveness: Performance in a Mediatized Culture* (2008), examines the tension between "liveness" and mediatization, but without repeating a perhaps intuitively obvious sequence: for Auslander, live performance does not come (temporally) prior to recording, nor can a theoretical prioritization of live performance over mediatized performative works be justified without qualification. In Auslander's view, the differences between live performances and medially mediated (or recorded) performances cannot be explained ontologically; instead, according to the historical understanding that makes it possible to speak of live performances in the first place, there is always a need for a counterpart in the form of mediatization.[10] This can be seen, for example, in the linguistic use of the term *live*, which only became meaningful when new communication technologies made human perception confused as to what it was dealing with. It was only through the technological possibility of live broadcasts, first on radio and then on television, that it became impossible to tell whether the images seen or the words heard were a live broadcast or prerecorded material. Live performances, then, have only ever existed in a media culture where there was at least the possibility of technical reproduction. Early television, in particular, with its promise of immediacy and intimacy, shaped the artistic medium of performance.[11] Following Auslander's conclusive arguments, the question of which contemporary forms of "liveness" are implemented in works such as DeLappe's *Elegy* becomes obvious.

Twitch, the streaming platform DeLappe chose for *Elegy*, evolved from justin.tv, a streaming start-up founded by Justin

Kan in 2007. Kan's original business model involved live streaming his life on the site twenty-four hours a day: blurry and out-of-focus images, as one would expect in the first decade of the twenty-first century, of a young man in his twenties who was repeatedly referred to as a "brogrammer." The aesthetics of the images of early streams on justin.tv, some of which have been "archived" on YouTube, show how underwhelming and inconsequential Justin's first-person reality TV stream was, despite his best efforts: although there are scenes in the archived footage of the solo entertainer striving to generate excitement, even Paul Graham, the investor and cofounder of Y Combinator, an American funding program central to the start-up scene, had to admit, "My first thought was that he spent an awful lot of time sleeping."[12]

Twitch was not designed from the outset for the live streaming of digital games but was instead intended as a stream "for everything," as justin.tv was. What is remarkable about the few screenshots of justin.tv that can still be found is the presence of a chat window next to the live-stream images. Immediacy and intimacy, the values Auslander used to define the so-called liveness of linear television, are also found here, supplemented by two new aspects: the audience's real-time communication with one other and with the person who is putting their life on display, and the possibility of directly intervening in the images through the comments in the chat—if the streamers want to react. Even if there is no convincing argument for corporeality in streamed performances on Twitch, the simultaneity of production and reception does not become less important. Rather, their interaction is enhanced by the possibility of real-time communication.

Image Performance and Performance Images

The concept of *real time* also characterizes computer game images: images of digital games must always be computed in real time in order to provide a continuous game experience. This circumstance connects performances in digital games with one of their historical predecessors: video performance. "When I first saw video feedback, I knew I had seen the cave fire," is how Woody Vasulka (who, with Steina Vasulka, founded The Kitchen in New York in 1971, a focus point for performance and video in the 1970s) described the fulcrum of video technology.[13] Performances in digital, streamed games differ a great deal from the video performances of the 1970s: in particular, analog video technology is overtly different from the digital, cloud-based imagery of contemporary games. However, they are united by one crucial feature: the manipulation of images in real time.

Video technology not only made working with moving images easier and more flexible than film by freeing them from large teams and heavy equipment; it also made it possible to view the images produced directly on a monitor with very low latency. The performers could thus react immediately to the images and interact with them.[14] According to Yvonne Spielmann, this enabled the new technology to create an artistic medium, since these conditions gave rise to a "specific aesthetic vocabulary" to develop, that of video performance.[15] Both formally and thematically, the possibility of video feedback spilled over into many of the artistic practices of the 1970s: this new quality of video technology enabled video performances in which live video was used as well as performances directly for and with the image. Formally, for example, Angela Washko's aforementioned project *The Council on Gender Sensitivity and Behavioral Awareness in World of Warcraft*, begun in 2012, could be seen as inheriting these new strategies from the late 1960s and 1970s.

Washko showed the work as a video, in which the artist, as an avatar in the MMORPG blockbuster game *World of Warcraft*, moves through the fantasy environment and begins conversations about gender and feminism with various other players or their avatars.[16] But she also presented the project as a live performance, in which she combined her actions with projected real-time images from *World of Warcraft*.

The reference to the historical legacy of video performance is meant to highlight two points: First, the same "aesthetic vocabulary" found in corporeal live performances should not be expected in live digital performances, since the respective technical possibilities interfere with their specific aesthetics. Second, video performances demonstrate that a notion of performance that focuses on action rather than corporeal presence is more fitting to these intermedial artistic actions and is anything but contradictory to the history of this medium. Kai van Eikels argues, especially in the case of early performances, for the supremacy of the execution character over the performance character: "With the emergence in the 1960s of an artistic movement that included 'performing' in its name *performance art*—the relationship between executing and performing as such became questionable. *Performance art* was not intended as an enactment art intended to stretch a theatrical constellation away from the stage on a cultural level; with it, an art of the performance of actions appeared, which precisely shifted the focus of artistic confrontation to that which, even in *theater performance*, was never completely absorbed into the particular format of the performance."[17]

The fact that execution acquires an intrinsic aesthetic value connects performances with the images of digital games. Computer game images are always performed or played: without actions, without the intervention in the proposed image worlds, and without playing the image, there are no computer games. Or, to use the words of Alexander Galloway: "Video games come into being when the machine is powered up and the software is executed, they exist when enacted. [...] With video games, the work itself is material action. One *plays* a game. And the software *runs*."[18] My point here is not to emphasize merely the image performativity of the interactive images of digital games, which would also miss my point about the conceptualization of performance as an artistic medium in streamed games. Rather, I want to point to the particular relationship of two meanings of the word *performance* that performances in streamed games engender: DeLappe's images always already bear witness to the performance of a technological infrastructure—that is, the implementation of actions because they are computer game images. But they are also performed, in another sense of the word—they are staged at a particular time (July 4, 2018–July 4, 2019), in a particular place (on Twitch). Thus, the choice of the performance venue is not an anti-institutional gesture toward the field of art; rather, it involves the use of a stage to achieve a specific, contemporary form of "liveness." The aforementioned artistic examples from digital, streamed games show that a performativization of the arts by no means goes hand in hand with a de-imaginization (*Entbildlichung*).[19] Rather, these examples are united by the fact that the performances build on the image performance of the interactive computer game image and are enabled by the performance conditions of streaming platforms. //

1   Sean O'Hagan, "Interview: Marina Abramović," *Guardian*, October 3, 2010, accessed February 25, 2022, www.theguardian.com/artanddesign/2010/oct/03/interview-marinaabramovic-performance-artist/.

2   In her performances *Rhythm 2* and *Rhythm 5*, in 1974, the artist was unconscious at times.

3   An avatar is the graphic representation of the player(s) in the game world. According to Benjamin Beil, avatars are characterized by the fact that they are not just a "*tool* for manipulating the game world, but also a *character* integrated into this game world," and by a minimum of narration and a certain "permanence of the player-avatar coupling" (italics in the original). The avatar concept thus enables active interaction with the game mechanics. Benjamin Beil, *Avatarbilder. Zur Bildlichkeit des zeitgenössischen Computerspiels* (Bielefeld: transcript Verlag, 2012), 9, 16. Translation by Natasha Pittet, Scribe Ltd.

4   Erika Fischer-Lichte, *Ästhetik des Performativen* (Frankfurt am Main: Suhrkamp, 2004).

5   "Performance cannot be saved, recorded, documented, or otherwise participate in the circulation of representations of representations: once it does so, it becomes something other than performance." Peggy Phelan, *Unmarked: The Politics of Performance* (New York and London: Routledge, 1993), 146.

6   See Judith Butler, "Performative Acts and Gender Constitution. An Essay in Phenomenology and Feminist Theory," *Theatre Journal* 40, no. 4 (December 1988): 519–31.

7   Fischer-Lichte, *Ästhetik des Performativen*, 47. Translation by Natasha Pittet, Scribe Ltd.

8   Her project *RMB City. A Second Life City Planning* (2007–11) was shown from 2008 to 2009 in the foyer of the Serpentine Gallery in London.

9   DeLappe was sourcing the data from the Gun Violence Archive; see Gun Violence Archive (website), accessed February 25, 2022, www.gunviolencearchive.org.

10   Philip Auslander, *Liveness: Performance in a Mediatized Culture* (New York and London: Routledge, 2008), 56.

11   Auslander, *Liveness*, 14–24.

12   Andrew Rice, "The Many Pivots of Justin.tv: How a Livecam Show Became Home to Video Gaming Superstars," *Fastcompany*, June 15, 2012, www.fastcompany.com/1839300/many-pivots-justintv-how-livecamshow-became-home-video-gaming-superstars/.

13   Quoted in Johanna Branson Gill, "Video. State of the Art," in *Eigenwelt der Apparatewelt. Pioniere der elektronischen Kunst / Pioneers of Electronic Art*, ed. Peter Weibel et al. (Linz and Santa Fe, NM: Ars Electronica and Vasulkas, 1992), 83.

14   Günter Berghaus, "From Video Art to Video Performance: The Work of Ulrike Rosenbach," in *Avant-Garde Film*, Avant-Garde Critical Studies, ed. Alexander Graf and Dietrich Scheunemann, vol. 23 (Amsterdam and New York: Rodopi, 2007), 321.

15   Yvonne Spielmann, "Video. From Technology to Medium," *Art Journal* 65, no. 3 (2006). 55.

16   MMORPG is the abbreviation for "massively multiplayer online role-playing game."

17   Kai van Eikels, *Die Kunst des Kollektiven. Performance zwischen Theater, Politik und Sozio-Ökonomie* (Paderborn: Wilhelm Fink, 2013), 21. Italics in the original. Translation by Natasha Pittet, Scribe Ltd.

18   Alexander R. Galloway, *Gaming: Essays on Algorithmic Culture*, Electronic Mediations, vol. 18 (Minneapolis: University of Minnesota Press, 2006), 2. Italics in the original.

19   See the discussion in Emmanuel Alloa, "Darstellen, was sich in der Darstellung allererst herstellt: Bildperformanz als Sichtbarmachung," in *Bild-Performanz*, ed. Ludger Schwarte (Munich and Paderborn: Fink, 2011), 34–39.

USE AND RECEPTION OF NEW MEDIA >>

#04

DIGITAL ART
AND THE QUANTIFICATION OF
AESTHETIC PERCEPTION

Aline Guillermet

The use of quantitative methodologies for qualitative purposes is at the core of recent debates about the relevance of the digital humanities in art history.[1] On the one hand, the digitization and scaling of analog methods may enable new connections and potentially new results, which could be crucial for the future development of the field.[2] These quantitative approaches, rather than militating against qualitative interpretations, may even provide new foundations. On the other hand, it is easy to imagine areas in which digital methods would fail to account for the complexity of their subject. While the computational approach to texts, also known as *distant reading*, has become central to literary studies in the last decade, a potential *distant viewing* would require that images be considered a visual language composed of discrete elements, amenable to quantification.[3] This presents a major challenge to digital art history. Among the many questions emerging from this new field of research, that of the quantification of aesthetic perception is of crucial importance.

When it comes to the visual arts, can the quantification of perception shed light on the processes of aesthetic appreciation? Recent research has addressed this question in two complementary ways. The first approach focuses on the human perception of works of art using a technique called *gaze tracking*. By recording and analyzing the eye movements of the observer, this approach aims to identify and understand perception patterns. A second approach uses image analysis and recognition (part of the broader field known as *computer vision*) in order to classify images according to predefined criteria. This second approach aims to develop new perceptual paradigms, potentially capable of generating "different points of inquiry than when observed only by the human eye," as media theorist Joanna Drucker has suggested.[4]

In parallel to their use in art history, gaze tracking and image recognition have recently been applied in contemporary digital art.[5] This is exemplified by a series of works of art using machine learning to question societal uses of digital technologies. As such, these artistic practices offer a prism through which to consider the methodological and philosophical difficulties raised by the application of digital methods to the field of art history. Digital art, this essay suggests, brings important critical perspectives to the recent debates outlined here. After providing some historical background to the quantification of aesthetic perception, I consider a selection of studies in digital art history in light of artistic practices using corresponding technologies, focusing on gaze tracking and on image recognition.

Buswell, Moles, and Information Aesthetics

When it comes to the visual arts, can the quantification of perception clarify processes of aesthetic appreciation? This question is neither new nor specific to twenty-first-century digital humanities. The first study of gaze movements applied to the perception of painting was carried out by Guy Thomas Buswell in 1935. Published in *How People Look at Pictures*, and based on 1,877 recordings made with two hundred participants, this study was the first to shed light on the unconscious eye movements that occur while a beholder looks at a specific painting.[6] Thanks to the graphical translation of visual pathways, Buswell also established patterns in the perceptual behavior of the participants and identified "centers of interest"—namely, areas where the gaze rests the most during the perception process.[7] Despite these groundbreaking results, Buswell remained extremely cautious about their qualitative application: "The present report does not treat in any manner the nature of the process of appreciation while looking at pictures. The evidence in regard to perceptual patterns is entirely objective, but it furnished no indication, except by inference, as to what the nature of the subject's inner response to the picture may be."[8]

Buswell's caution expresses a fundamental difficulty inherent in any attempt at deductive logic in science: measuring an outcome (here, the perception) is one thing, but it is quite another to discover the cause of this outcome (what Buswell calls "the nature of the process of appreciation"). However, the broader cross-disciplinary impact of these results remained minor, as one commentator of the time remarked rather ungenerously, "Nothing of the slightest importance to the science of aesthetics or psychology seems to result from this research."[9]

By the end of the 1950s, a new European movement revived these questions. Pioneered by philosopher Max Bense in Germany and physicist Abraham Moles in France, information aesthetics sought to bridge the gap between the quantitative and the qualitative spheres. Situated at the convergence of information theory, psychology, and philosophy, this new discipline aimed to establish a scientific basis for the study of art by applying theoretical principles derived from information sciences, particularly those of Claude Shannon's information theory, to the creation and perception of works of art. For Moles, the visual arts were a "form of communication"—namely, a language whose discrete elements can be measured statistically.[10]

Fundamentally, informational aesthetics aimed to extract aesthetics from its metaphysical tradition in order to rebuild it scientifically. According to this new approach, beauty would be linked to objective properties that were "statistically demonstrable" and could be "experimentally tested."[11] In 1971, in line with this agenda, Moles imagined a future in which "emotion engineers" would soon be able to "program [aesthetic] pleasure."[12]

Half a century later, the rise of artificial intelligence appears to further blur the distinction between algorithmic and human processes. Machine learning has enabled language generation software to perform tasks that mimic human creativity, such as writing fiction and poetry. Depending on what corpus it "learns," this kind of software can also simulate—if not "program"—human emotions, as the digital artwork *Empathy Deck* (2016–17) demonstrates. Designed by Greek artist Erica Scourti in collaboration with Tom Armitage, this "robot with feelings" is programmed to send personalized comforting messages to its Twitter followers. In this case, the algorithm was given the artist's personal diaries as a corpus to train with, which resulted in a mix of pseudo-intimate confessions and self-help advice **Fig. 1**. Given these new technological possibilities, how do the quantitative studies of human perception that interest us negotiate the disciplinary divide that Moles had hoped to overcome?

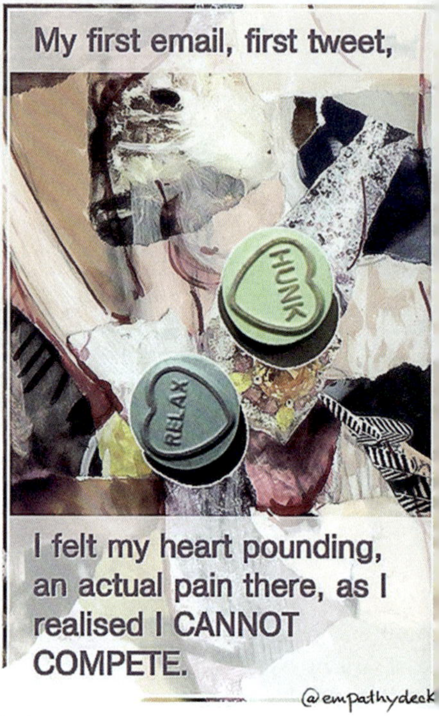

Fig. 1

Fig. 1 Erica Scourti, generated card from *Empathy Deck*, 2016–17.

Perceiving a Painting: From Diderot to Digital Painting

The study of gaze movements as applied to the perception of painting has a famous forerunner. During the eighteenth century, French philosopher Denis Diderot hypothesized about a "line of liaison," a formal feature of a painting that guides the gaze and, as such, shapes the viewer's aesthetic experience.[13] A study conducted by the Laboratory for Cognitive Research in Art History at the University of Vienna recently reexamined this hypothesis. The authors showed digital reproductions of two paintings discussed by Diderot to a group of forty observers.[14] The data collected indicated the individual paths of perception and were organized into periods of fixation on areas of interest and into saccades (the brief and extremely rapid movements of the gaze from one area of interest to another). An algorithm calculated the number of transitions made by eye saccades between each area. The authors drew two conclusions from this study: while "Diderot's analyses [...] do not match the real dynamic of the eye" (Buswell had already reached this conclusion in 1935), "his description of a line of composition in Vien's altarpiece is correct as long as we consider the frequently repeated saccades and not the actual course of the movement of the eye."[15] In other words, the quantitative analysis of gaze movements confirms and refines Diderot's intuition. These conclusions are relatively modest, even disappointing. As Michael Baxandall had already noted when considering the perception patterns of Georges Braque's *Violin and Pitcher*, "the fixations generally confirm expectations."[16] Moreover, they fail to reveal anything about what Buswell called the "nature of the subject's inner response to the picture." In light of these recent studies applying quantitative methods to human perception, one question remains to be asked: What conceptual model(s) would enable a mediation between the data and its interpretation?

This question informs a series of recent works by Swedish artist Jonas Lund. In 2013, Lund designed *Gallery Analytics* for the exhibition "Momentum" in The Hague. This site-specific installation analyzed the personal Wi-Fi signal of each visitor in order to track their progress in the exhibition space in real time. The data thus collected yielded information on the total number of visitors and on the average time that each visitor spent in the exhibition and in front of each artwork. According to the artist, similar tracking devices have been used in shopping malls to rank the display windows according to popularity.[17] By transposing this experiment to an art-gallery context, Lund exposes the flawed model underpinning the marketing uses of tracking technology, according to which duration of contemplation is interpreted as having a higher "quantity" of interest, and asks anew, "What does the fact that a visitor

Fig. 2

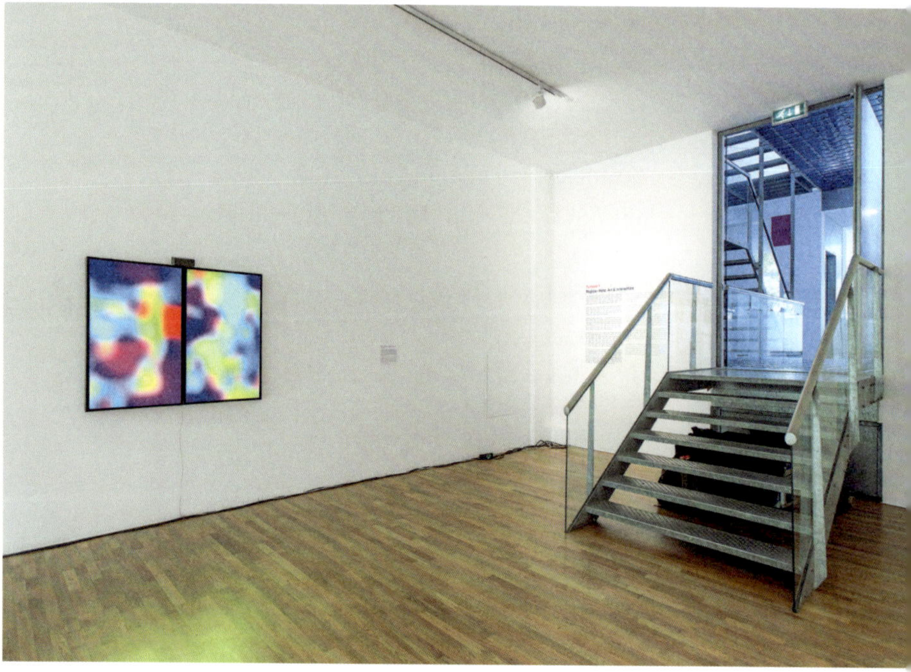

spends more time in front of one work than an-other signify?"[18]

In another work, entitled *VIP (Viewer Improved Painting)*, from 2014, Lund brings this question to bear on the perception of a digital "painting": two brightly colored screens are hung vertically, side by side **Fig. 2**. Located between the two screens, a camera records the be-holder's gaze. An algorithm processes the recorded data using the preference evaluation method known as "A/B testing." If the observer looks at one screen, the algorithm will take this "preference" into account by deleting the content of the oth-er screen from its database. Initially, each screen is mono-chromatic. In response to the data collected by the central camera, each surface slowly morphs into a digital color field painting, with pink, blue, purple, and green accents. Although the installation records the beholder's "preference" for one screen over another, it does not respond in real time. In other words, the link between the data collected by the camera and the resulting pictorial combinations is indirect and does not satisfy a specific beholder's tastes. As its title indicates, *VIP* is "improved" by the "viewer," but this viewer is no one in particu-lar, somewhere between Hume's "man in general," aiming for an empirical "standard of taste," and a disembodied, statistical aggregate of beholders. If, as I suggest, a model does underpin *VIP*, it is a problematic one: namely, the hypothesis that a work of art could improve in general rather than improve for the in-dividual human subject.

Fig. 2 Jonas Lund, *VIP (Viewer Improved Painting)*, 2014, self-optimizing digital painting, fifty-inch-monitor TV, custom metal frame, gaze tracking camera, installation view, Foam Foto-grafiemuseum, Amsterdam.

Perceiving a Painting: Computer Vision

The development of computational image recognition and its recent application to the history of art have opened up a second approach to quantifying the perception of works of art. Metaphorically called *computer vision,* it uses machine learning to identify formal links within a given corpus. In art history, applications range from the structural analysis of individual works to the comparison and classification of patterns across a selection of works. So far, digital image recognition has mainly served to automate analog processes, making large-scale comparisons possible. These often-successful applications challenge the strict opposition between the quantitative and the qualitative spheres: as Drucker notes, the change of scale itself can potentially produce a "radically different" effect.[19]

However, image recognition poses two challenges to art history. The first is generic and concerns the very nature of computer vision. A brief consideration of recognition software is enough to see that what is called computer "vision" is, in fact, a formal recognition process, which relies on prior programming and learning. The second, more specific, challenge concerns the nature of the object of study and whether its formal structure lends itself to quantification, a necessary condition for algorithmic processing.

The digital humanities are well aware of this challenge: existing studies in distant viewing require a thorough analysis of the object of study prior to making any further methodological decisions pertaining to its quantification. A recent study of Aby Warburg's *Pathosformeln* (pathos formulas) demonstrates this point.[20] Following a conceptual analysis that highlights the importance of the body—as opposed to the face—in the expression of pathos in Warburg's examples, the authors, Leonardo Impett and Franco Moretti, transform the concept of *Pathosformeln* into "a series of quantifiable operations, thus turning it into an instrument to actually measure the objects it refers to."[21] They conceive of the quantification of the images according to three methodological principles: (1) removing the human figures from their original context; (2) reducing their bodies to skeletons; (3) measuring only one variable, namely the angles formed by the body's joints, now outlined by vectors.[22] Reducing the objects of study (a series of representations of men and women) to the low-dimensional space of vectors makes it possible for the algorithm to "see" and classify these objects. According to Impett and Moretti, the algorithm was able to identify and isolate all the figures associated with *Pathosformeln* by Warburg. They conclude that their analysis opens the way to "an enlargement of the *Mnemosyne* project well beyond what Warburg had himself been able to do."[23]

In short, Impett and Moretti's study argues that the algorithm could perform the same tasks as Warburg but on a larger scale. However, does it also support the claim that algorithmic perception "sees" aspects hitherto imperceptible to the human eye?[24] In the study of *Pathosformeln*, what the algorithm "saw" is controversial. Contrary to the authors' expectations, all occurrences of pathos, although correctly identified, were grouped together in the same category by the algorithm, putting on the same plane a series of images with extremely varied iconographic content: a nymph bearing a plate of fruits, the priest agonizing at the center of the sculpted group of the *Laocoön*, and Judith's maid carrying the severed head of Holofernes. For Impett and Moretti, "clearly, the algorithm had 'seen' a similarity among the *Pathosformeln* skeleton vectors, which seemed to consist in this: *Pathosformeln* were all correlated to a *simultaneous movement of both arms and legs* [...]. This was the shared morphological feature around which the algorithm had clustered *Pathosformeln* together."[25] Although at first surprising, this clustering indicates only one thing: namely, that the algorithm did what it was asked to do and took the numerical value of the angles formed by the position of the figures' arms and legs as its basis for classification. Finally, as far as the results' "anthropological or aesthetic meaning," the authors concede that they "feel [...] in the dark."[26]

The Visual Genome (2019), a two-channel video installation featuring computational analyses of images by British artist Toby Ziegler, echoes this concern.[27] Ziegler's video presents a succession of images analyzed by computer vision and sub-titled with their textual description [Fig. 3]. To achieve this, *The Visual Genome* appropriates an eponymous image-recognition tool produced by a team of researchers based at Stanford University. The innovation of the *Visual Genome* software lies in its capacity, beyond simple pattern recognition, to analyze the relationships that structure the image (background and form, container and content, types of activity, etc.) and to generate corresponding linguistic descriptions [Fig. 4].

Fig. 3

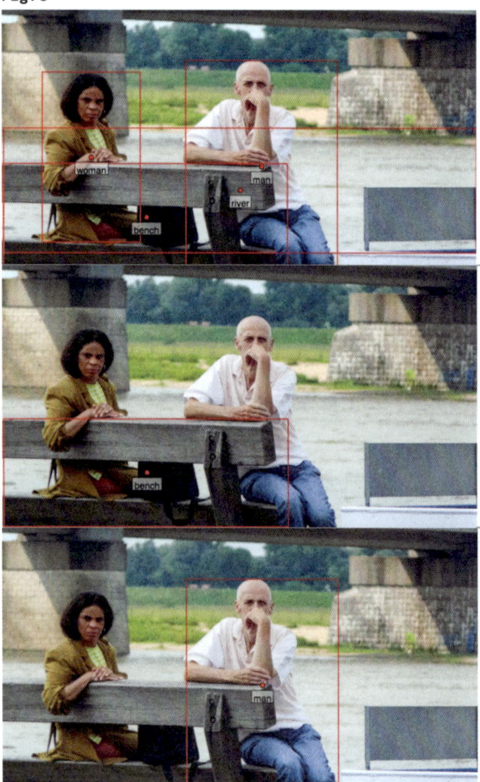

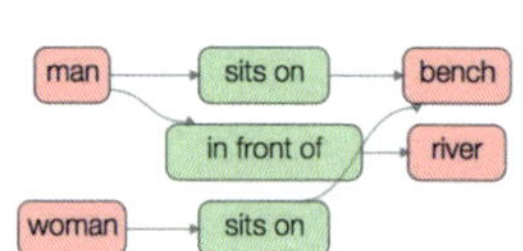

A man and a woman sit on a park bench along a river.

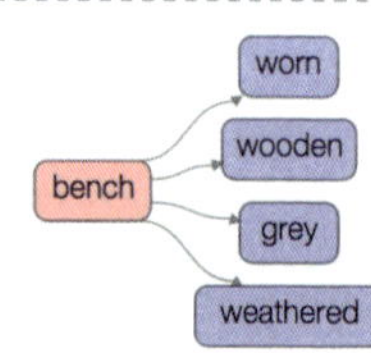

Park bench is made of gray weathered wood

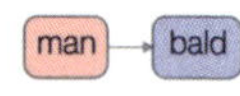

The man is almost bald

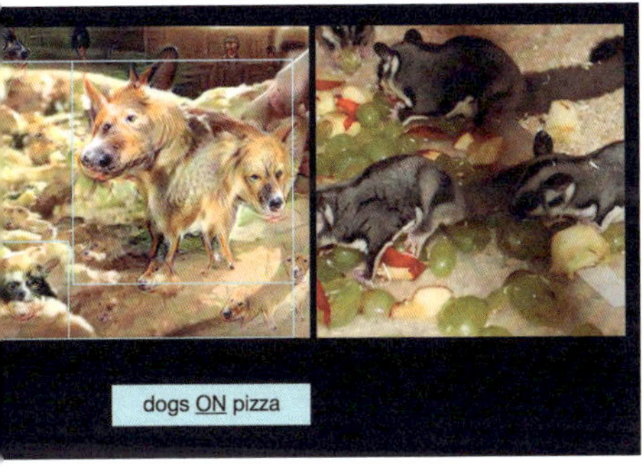

Fig. 4

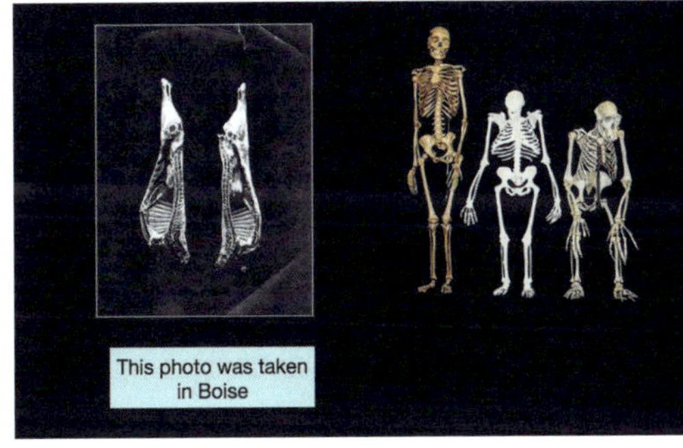

Fig. 5

However, in Ziegler's video some of the subtitles associated with the images, such as "pastry is breakfast," "this photo is great," or "this photo was taken in Boise," evoke subjective value judgements more than objective descriptions Fig. 5. These did not originate in the computer program but, rather, were added by Ziegler himself. Arguably, these tongue-in-cheek artistic interventions expose the danger of a possible shift from objective processing of data to subjective processes of interpretation. Art historians, we might therefore conclude, should treat seeming conclusions resulting from automated image perception with the utmost caution. At the same time, they should also guard against the situation, which Claire Bishop deplored in her polemical article "Against Digital Art History," in which "the task of interpreting these patterns is left up to others."[28]

Faced with the problem of a methodological break between quantitative and qualitative approaches, art history can draw some lessons from the works of Lund, Scourti, and Ziegler. Between techno art and science fiction, the artists use advanced technologies in their practices with the ultimate goal of repositioning the human subject at the center of their discourse. The prism of digital art, therefore, highlights the importance of a critique, in the Kantian sense of delimiting the field of application, of the use of computational methods in

Fig. 3 Example from the *Visual Genome database*, 2017, published in Krishna, Zhu et al., "Visual Genome," 35.

Figs. 4, 5 Toby Ziegler, screenshot from *The Visual Genome*, 2019, two-channel video installation, 4:19.

art history. This caution is all the more necessary in studies of the aesthetic perception of works of art that, despite the growing effectiveness of methods of gaze tracking and computer vision, still resists quantification. As Buswell suggested, more work needs to be undertaken on mediating between objective data and its subjective interpretation, if digital methods are to enlighte "the nature of the process of appreciation while looking at pictures."[29] //

1 See Claire Bishop's polemical essay, "Against Digital Art History," *Humanities Future*, 2015, http://humanitiesfutures.org/papers/digital-art-history/.

2 This is Joanna Drucker's argument in "Is There a 'Digital' Art History?," *Visual Resources* 29, nos. 1–2 (2013): 5–13.

3 The term *distant reading* was coined by Franco Moretti in 2000 and originally referred to a predigital quantitative approach to literature; see Franco Moretti, "Conjectures on World Literature," *New Left Review* 1 (2000): 54–68. The term now refers to computational analyses; see Andrew Goldstone, "The *Doxa* of Reading," *PMLA* 132, no. 3 (2017): 636.

4 Drucker, "Is There a 'Digital' Art History?," 8.

5 In her landmark survey, Christiane Paul defines digital art as "produced, stored, and presented exclusively in the digital format": Paul, *Digital Art* (London: Thames and Hudson), 2003, 8.

6 Guy Thomas Buswell, *How People Look at Pictures* (Chicago: University of Chicago Press, 1935).

7 Buswell uses the term "centers of interest," but "areas of interest" is now more commonly used in psychology.

8 Buswell, *How People Look at Pictures*, 10.

9 Quoted in Raphael Rosenberg and Christoph Klein, "The Moving Eye of the Beholder: Eye Tracking and the Perception of Paintings," in *Art, Aesthetics and the Brain*, ed. Joseph P. Huston et al. (Oxford: Oxford University Press, 2015), 79–108, at 89.

10 Abraham Moles, *Art et ordinateur* (Paris: Casterman, 1971), 15. Translation by the author.

11 Moles, *Art et ordinateur*, 15.

12 Moles, *Art et ordinateur*, 130.

13 Denis Diderot, "The Salon of 1767," in *Diderot on Art*, vol. 2, trans. John Goodman (New Haven, CT: Yale University Press, 1995), 29.

14 *St. Denis Preaching in Gaul* (1767) by Joseph-Marie Vien, and *The Miracle of the Ardents* (1767) by Gabriel François Doyen.

15 Rosenberg and Klein, "The Moving Eye," 94–95.

16 Michael Baxandall, "Fixation and Distraction: The Nail in Braque's *Violin and Pitcher* (1910)," in *Sight and Insight. Essays on Art and Culture in Honour of E. H. Gombrich at 85*, ed. John Onians (London: Phaidon, 1994), 409.

17 See "Gallery Analytics," accessed March 10, 2023, https://jonaslund.com/works/gallery-analytics/.

18 Jonas Lund, video conversation with the author, November 5, 2020.

19 Drucker, "Is There a 'Digital' Art History?," 10.

20 Brought together in Warburg's *Bilderatlas Mnemosyne*, the examples of *Pathosformeln* are bodily expressions of intense psychological states collected across a range of visual cultures. The study mentioned is Leonardo Impett and Franco Moretti, "Totentanz: Operationalizing Aby Warburg's Pathosformeln," *New Left Review* 107, no. 1 (2017): 68–97.

21 Impett and Moretti, "Totentanz," 71.

22 Impett and Moretti, "Totentanz," 78–80.

23 Impett and Moretti, "Totentanz," 93.

24 Drucker argues that this is the case, as shown in a study led by Antonio Criminisi, Martin Kemp, and Andrew Zisserman in 2005, whose analyses of models of perspective in painting demonstrated "deviation from mathematically perfect models of perspective." Quoted in Drucker, "Is There a 'Digital' Art History?," 10.

25 Impett and Moretti, "Totentanz," 94. Italics in the original.

26 Impett and Moretti, "Totentanz," 96.

27 On this artwork, see Aline Guillermet, "Seeing Outside the Box," in *Soft Power: Mosso, Morandi, Ziegler* (Milan: Tommaso Calabro Galeria, 2019), 36–38. The video is available online; see *The Visual Genome*, accessed March 10, 2023, http://vimeo.com/327667499/.

28 Bishop, "Against Digital Art History."

29 Buswell, *How People Look at Pictures*, 10.

#05

SOFTWARE GARDEN: LIFE IN DIGITAL MATTER

Nina Zschocke

(with a visual contribution by U5)

Theater Neumarkt, Zurich, Saturday, September 26, 2020

Empty seats separate us, masks are worn to lower infection risk, half of the auditorium is roped off: social distancing rules. Nevertheless, you can feel the excitement in the room: Rory Pilgrim's *Software Garden* can be performed onstage, despite the Covid-19 pandemic. The stage is flanked by seats on two sides, a computer monitor, and a large projection screen. Pilgrim's multimedia production is the result of a three-day workshop at the neighboring Cabaret Voltaire. Moreover, it is part of a series of collaborative works taking place since 2016, including music videos, concerts, and an exhibition. This afternoon, eight workshop participants are performing together with dancer and choreographer Cassie Augusta Jørgensen, accompanied by singer Robyn Haddon and harpist Pilgrim. The dance and music performance on-site is combined with the live video appearance on-screen of poet and disability advocate Carol R. Kallend.[1] Other prerecorded videos are also projected. In fall 2020, this combination of on- and offline contributions, of live and prerecorded content, and of telepresence and performance on-site resonates with the audience's experience. After half a year of online meetings, video conferences, digital dial-ins from quarantine, home office, or remote workation retreats, the presence of technical equipment and gadgets seems more common and more natural than the proximity of other people. The monitor onstage is familiar. As usual, cables snake across the floor. We are all accustomed to technical communication problems. Pilgrim is the "host" of this "meeting." He coordinates all contributions and operates various devices.

On-screen, Kallend, who is from Sheffield, England, recites her own poetry. Speaking as a person living with physical disabilities, Kallend expresses in her poem the wish to have a robot by her side: a robot as an aide; a robot as a companion; a robot replacing a nurse; a robot as substitute for absent human care. Technology is addressed here as a last resort, in the hope of softening the blow of the British austerity program—a series of severe pension and subsidy cuts enforced since 2010. Kallend does not voice accusations or political claims but gently speaks of a longing and attempts to make tender contact with a humanoid device in prerecorded video sequences.[2]

A similar twist, a related turning away from open political struggle toward the fragile, vulnerable dreaming of alternative futures, is expressed in an interview by Pilgrim in 2017. Here, the artist explained that, as a queer person, he devised a kind of survival instinct and activist drive "not to give up." However, instead of devoting all his energy to critique and to the exhausting fight against power, Pilgrim said that in his art practice, he wished to leave space for optimistic imaginaries.[3] It is in this context that digital technologies are allowed to appear onstage as components of safe and caring hybrid communal spaces, yet to be built.

As much as Pilgrim and Kallend's dream of encountering digital devices as strange yet friendly cohabitants and making them kin is reminiscent of Donna Haraway's famous 1985 feminist *Cyborg Manifesto,* this appears irritatingly naive in 2020. Wishing for a "monstrous world without gender," Haraway saw the chance in the 1980s in feminist appropriations of biotech-

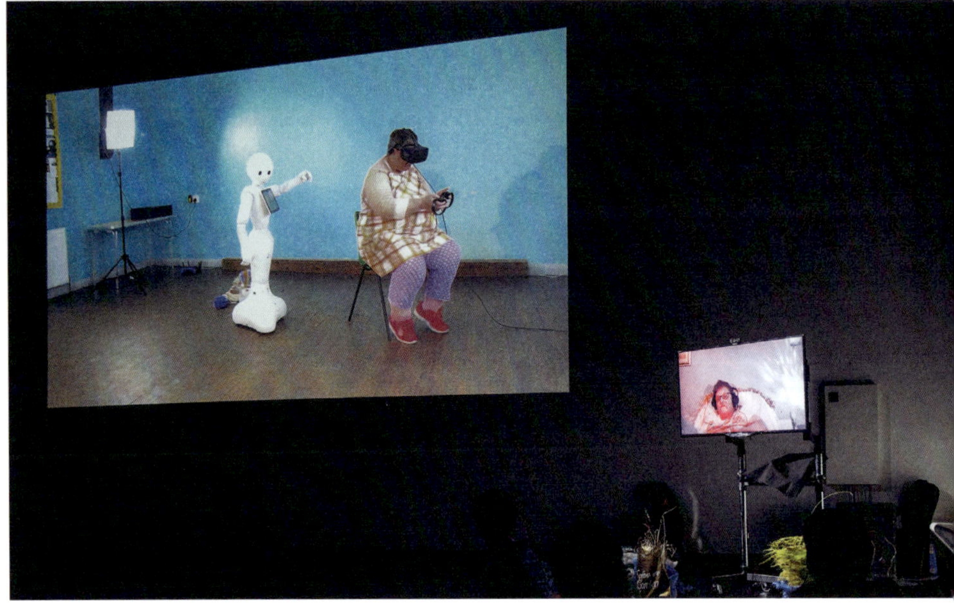

Fig.1

nology and microelectronics to subvert dualistic models of gender as well as distinctions between the human and nonhuman, including machines.[4] Forty years later, we know that exploitative—capitalist, patriarchal, colonial—structures as well as norms and prejudices are being inscribed into digital technologies, including communication platforms and personal devices.[5] Yet, in view of this critical discourse as well as negative experience and frustration, Pilgrim nevertheless made the decision to deliberately not direct attention toward the corruptions of current software and hardware in favor of giving space to a cautiously optimistic imaginary life, an alternative narrative. One reason is the perceived urgency to productively engage with technologies that, harmful as they may be, are already shaping reality today or that threaten to do so in the near future. Precisely because research institutions and companies are developing so-called care robots, there is a need to some-

Fig.1 Rory Pilgrim, *Software Garden* 2019, live concert, Stedelijk Museum, Amsterdam.

Fig.2 Rory Pilgrim, *Software Garden* 2016–18, HD video (still), 52:30.

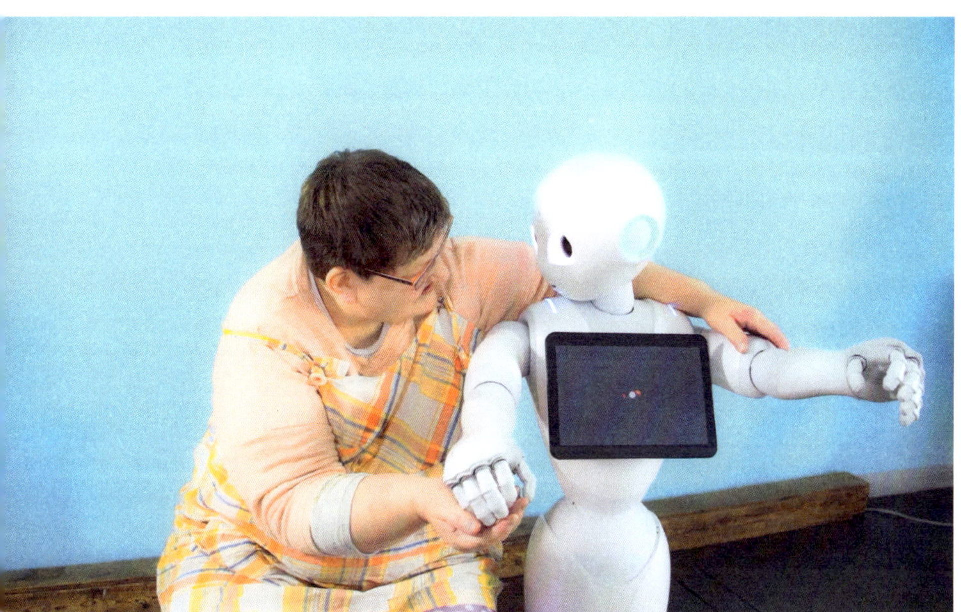

Fig. 2

how get involved. Pilgrim says, "A tangible example of the huge
segment of research into robotics is based on how robots can
be carers for people. [...] With an ageing population the reality
of having robots adopting a caring role is becoming ever more
likely. I think we need to have the spaces to think about these
changes and be conscious of the issues this raises."[6]

In the video sequences projected onstage, Carol Kallend
interacts with a Pepper-type robot [Figs. 1, 2]. This humanoid ap-
paratus, codeveloped by French and Japanese companies and
first introduced in 2014, was "designed to live with humans."[7] It
runs on rollers and can move its arms and head, detect human
presence through visual face recognition, read some expressions and gestures as emotions, understand a limited set of
questions, and react with programmed behaviors and visual
and audio output. It indicates its state (listening, processing,
not activated) through the changing color of its eyes. Pepper
comes with a touch screen, microphone, camera, and audio

output. Equipped with Wi-Fi, it can be regarded as comparable to a smart home device, armed with a robotic body. Far from being able to do physical care work, the robot seems to have been tested mainly for simple entertainment use in retirement homes.[8] The robot tells jokes or reads stories, and games can be played, activated through a tablet computer attached to the robot's upper body. Kallend's interaction with Pepper was filmed in collaboration with the robotics department at the University of Sheffield, which develops "robotic platforms and systems for healthcare and assistive living."[9] On-screen, we see a human-machine performance, which avoids any of the robot's entertainment functions. These are staged moments of making contact, hesitant touch, and attempted imitation between human and machine—gestures expressing the hope of moving toward intuitive, tender, future encounters. Is this performance, which apparently refuses to recognize the various interests hidden behind the robot's smooth surface and big eyes, an optimistic kind of science fiction?

Dystopian science fiction from Isaac Asimov to H. G. Wells (and on to Sibylle Berg or Chen Qiufan) shows the abysses of the present as scenarios for the future. In turn, radically optimistic sci-fi continues to spread through commercials, business plans, and strategy papers—glowing with optimism, keeping up the technological promise of innovation and salvation. Company vision, mission statement, TED talk. "In one way or another, from Plato on, utopia has been the big yang motorcycle trip. Bright, dry, clear, strong, firm, active, aggressive, lineal, progressive, creative, expanding, advancing, and hot," argues Ursula K. Le Guin.[10] However, Le Guin sees great value in speculative fiction whenever it takes the form of a thought experiment, when it is more question than answer, and when it appears as process rather than definitive solution: "One of the essential functions of science fiction, I think, is precisely this kind of question-asking: reversals of an habitual way of thinking, metaphors for what our language has no words for as yet, experiments in imagination."[11]

Donna Haraway's related concept of "staying with the trouble" is opposed to "a cosmic faith in technofixes," yet it also stands against the belief that "the game is over, it's too late, there is no sense trying to make anything any better."[12] Pilgrim's work might be in this lineage. Is he hinting at a future where robots and other digital technologies, freed from the reign of a liberal economy, form alliances with the weak, the powerless, and those in need? Is he painting the picture of sensuous encounters with digital devices as nonhuman cohabitants in a fantastically fertile *Software Garden*? Performing a dream, telling a story differently, or a different story? On closer look, Kallend's cautious attempts to contact an electronic companion are deeply unsettling—both because we know that they originate from desperation and because they are doomed to fail. The performers sing—and Pilgrim speaks—about "post-love": "a love that is felt by the inanimate, the mechanical, the robotic, animals, plants and humans."[13] Yet, the encounter between Kallend and the nonhuman, inanimate Pepper cannot last. Kallend is not a mystically cyborgian Björk in "All Is Full of Love" but a real person, trying in vain to make meaningful contact with a machine.[14] All this is present: the dream of new connections, on the one hand, and the nightmare of dismantled welfare, on the other; a lonely person keeping up hope while being confronted with tech companies that target emerging markets; third-party money-shaping research groups; money invested not in higher wages for nurses but in profitable technical solutions. Unable to counter such forces, Kallend appears onstage as a vulnerable figure, exploring what is left for her—or what might come. We see someone in distress, trustingly approaching technology, because there might soon be nothing and nobody else she can turn to. Even if Pilgrim is staging a collaborative process with an essentially optimistic point of departure, human tragedy remains through Kallend's poem and video robot performance. This perceived ambivalence appears to superimpose two forms of critique: the dream of an alternative world as implicit criticism of the status quo and the demonstration of real, specific traps and deficiencies.

Pilgrim and his group use not a robot but other, more conventional digital tools to telecollaborate. While the performance moves on at the theater, Kallend remains present via a live video connection. When the group on-site dance together, she watches silently—from the other end of the communication channel. From the start of the *Software Garden* series, videoconferencing has been the technical means for Kallend's participation. In this sense, the project builds a temporary multimedia space allowing for inclusive collaboration. Thus, while in the interaction with a robotic "mindless agent," compassion must remain fiction, on the level of interhuman telecollaboration, proximity between the performers, musicians, and poet is, to a certain extent, achieved through digital media.[15] What Pilgrim presents is no utopian science fiction: not a perfect world but rather frictions, ruptures, and open questions—questions concerning the future of care work as well as interhuman and human-machine relations in the digital age.

On the one hand, Kallend's contribution highlights the situation of people experiencing isolation, social deprivation, and a lack of physical and emotional assistance much more directly, severely, and painfully than many of us. On the other, her precarious situation as a care-dependent person is situated within and results from broader sociocultural, political, and technological shifts. Paying attention to Kallend's position helps to put some of these changes in a new light. Moreover, through the topic of care, *Software Garden* exemplifies the more general challenges of critiquing the current state of digital media while at the same time having to use some of the advantages of its technologies.

ETH Zurich, Online and Hybrid Teaching, Fall 2020

It is the 2020 fall semester: lecture classes are taught online, via the private videoconferencing platform Zoom. Standing alone in an empty auditorium to transmit and record my lecture during the Covid-19 crisis, I can—despite my comparatively very privileged position—easily relate to aspects of Kallend's situation. I can relate to the tension between the hope that technology will somehow help to manage a crisis and a strong feeling of loss. There is also tension between the successful use of, for example, videoconferencing formats and doubts about the trustworthiness of the applications in question. The universal design of videoconferencing interfaces demonstrates smooth functioning—speaker view, gallery view, screen sharing. Beatriz Colomina and Mark Wigley see a connection between the modern ideology of "good design" as smoothness and the design of the smartphone: smooth surfaces, no friction, no sensation.[16] The image space of videoconferencing exhibits similar properties, especially when used in standardized settings or with virtual backgrounds. A seminar starts to resemble a business or a Covid meeting, an EU conference, or the G20 summit. Interaction via screens remains reduced, somewhat rudimentary, with dimensions lost. These are maximally controlled media spaces that do everything to lock us in.

For other courses—in particular, a collectively taught intensive writing seminar led by Philip Ursprung, chair of the history of art and architecture at ETH Zurich—we decide to switch to hybrid modes of teaching outdoors: meetings in person, combined with online formats.[17] Some of us meet in front of the university building. The outdoor space protects us from infection; a projecting roof, from rain. We sit in winter clothes and blankets, computers on our knees. Together with the art collective U5, we experiment with how to use digital networks to benefit inclusion during the pandemic while, simultaneously, preventing the group from sinking and disappearing entirely into the blue light of computer screens.[18] Methods vary: producing unorthodox connections and allowing for breaks, disruptions, and intensifying experiences and encounters in person. The goals: to tame the precision of programming; to keep the relations between concepts and phenomena unstable; to produce situations suitable for catching something still unexpected or unfamiliar.[19]

Right there, in front of our department building, leaves fall, sunbeams shine, an esoteric ritual is playfully tested, tea is brewed and shared, feet freeze, and batteries die. Extension cables are installed, a boombox gives volume to distant voices, we learn how to avoid feedback loops, it gets too cold, and construction noise rumbles in the background. We move and carry chairs, blankets, computers, and cables. On-screen, a baby is being fed. It is a privilege to meet on campus. And it is hugely lucky that digital windows open up this campus to other spaces, to isolation chambers—or to a young mother's home. We discover that our hybrid settings teach us to think and act collectively and to remember to include those not present, those who need technical support to be heard. We learn that it is not possible to fully focus on the here and now, there is always an elsewhere, and there are fragile connections to attend to.

One semester later, with the next seminar, we continue to meet outside, sometimes off campus, in the city, visiting buildings or public artworks.[20] We use street furniture for hours of reading and discussion. Always with us are a laptop, camera,

Fig. 3 On-/offline hybrid teaching experiment on-site for the course "Exhibit Inhabit," Department of Architecture, ETH Zurich, spring 2021.

and microphone for participation via the video channel. This is not the prescribed online teaching. But we are conforming to official Covid rules: group size, contact tracing, fresh air. This is a conspiracy to not give up what we love. It is passion for—and belief in the didactic values of—explorative field work, direct experience, informal intellectual exchange, and social interaction [Fig. 3].

Together, we ask ourselves: Which possibilities and spaces for collaboration remain in pandemic times? Where are the blind spots and gaps in the university guidelines, terrains to be explored? How can we remain creative in teaching art and architectural history? What are the old and new methods and tools at hand? How can we continue to meet our students in person—and have them meet each other—without becoming exclusive or taking health risks? How can we avoid teleworking in isolation and continue to improvise together? How can we produce temporary, fragile connections and avoid overprivileging homogenous virtual spaces? Or do we need to capture more

Fig. 3

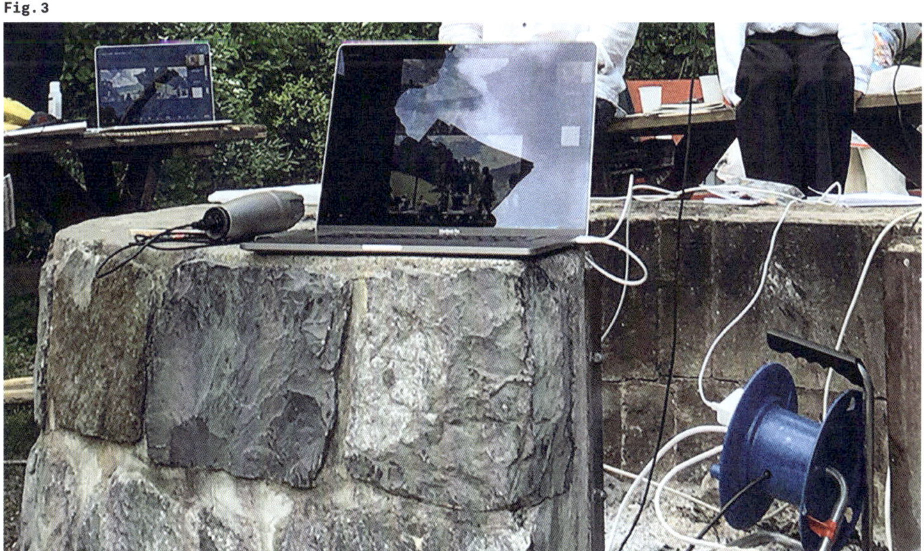

of the situation on-site? Are we dreaming of multidimensional tools, transmitting material qualities, spatial relations, physical textures, odors? Or is there too much data already: facial expressions, voices, emotions, content, friends, colleagues, teachers, bedroom, office, studio, lab, seminar room, street, bus, beach, public space, other people. Data consuming energy, data needing infrastructure, shaping space—all that data. Thus, the ambivalences we face relate to those staged by Rory Pilgrim: live video produces inclusiveness; it allows for participation in a social process, being a member of a group. Yet, the tools we use feed data to private companies. We were forced out of the heterotopia of a university that is public and operates in public space. Instead: private digital platforms. What kind of experiences point toward these critical issues and trigger a critical discussion within the group?

Aran Islands, Ireland, March 2019

It is seminar week for the Department of Architecture at ETH Zurich. A group of students and the faculty is exploring Inisheer, the smallest of the Irish Aran Islands, together with the artist collective U5. With us, we have twenty-five of U5's PALM cameras, clipped to backpacks, pants' pockets, shoes, and bicycle handlebars.[21] While we turn our attention to the variety of dry-stone wall techniques or to a performance by artist Isabel Nolan, each camera takes a picture every two seconds. Pictures of whatever happens appear. The screenless cameras attached to us transmit the images, unseen, to a server and website hosted by U5. The flow of automatic data is not accessible to us, at least not immediately. And if these cameras are perception prostheses, then they are certainly not ours. Do these many networked eyes turn us into a "swarm" with a new type of collective sensibility—or have we been infested by digital parasites?

Before crossing to the Aran Islands off the coast of Ireland, we passed the landing point of the transatlantic cable, a major link in the material infrastructure of global Internet traffic. We also walked around Google and Microsoft data centers on the outskirts of Dublin. Through high fences, we spied the opaque facades of storage facilities, overflowing with digital gold. Uninvited and somewhat perplexed, we stood in front of the built manifestations of companies that, having declared the digital records of human behavior to be a freely accessible resource, have grown rich using their users' data, including ours. These are the treasure chests and monuments of platform capitalism, of surveillance capitalism.[22]

The PALM Cam project by U5, in which we and the students engage on the fieldtrip, seems to echo—on a much smaller scale—certain structural aspects of the self-enrichment systems characterizing platform capitalism. Participation requires acceptance of an opaque black-box device. An autonomous sensory system enters our daily lives. We engage in the unpaid production of images that will circulate online. Taking part in U5's project means contributing to an accumulation of material. PALM ensures that U5 has access to an inexhaustible data stream it can process and use in its work. Trusting U5 also means accepting that you may pop up in an exhibition space, caught on photo in an odd pose, covered with glued-on beads.

On April 5, 2019, two weeks after the swarm experiment in Ireland, the streams from the twenty-five cameras go online on the PALM platform and on a screen in U5's studio. The flood of five hundred thousand automatic images contains unexpected perspectives, which are often at odds with our perceptions and memories. Many of the motifs seem trivial or unimportant—legs, feet, the ground, the insides of bags, close-ups of stones, visual noise—but there are also landscapes, the sky, people, buildings, all in multiple variations; some cameras

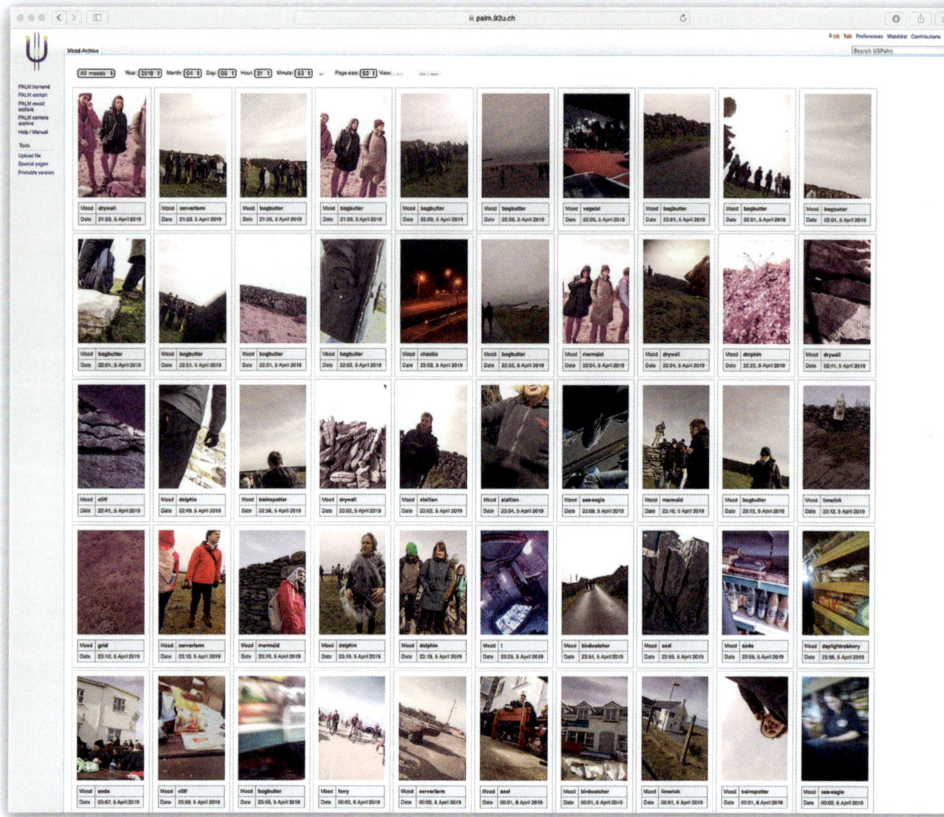

Fig. 4

transmit black voids, while others produce images tinged with magenta. We are invited to attach meaning to selected images via the emotional keyword option on the web page. However, this activity does not produce classifications with any obvious use. Is there a logic to the available terms? Do they fulfill a hidden purpose? Engaging with U5's PALM project on a study trip raises questions instead of providing answers: Is this surveillance or a social game? Is this management or a creative process? How should we handle big data? Who has access? Do digital devices serve me, or I them? How do devices alter our perceptions and relationships? Which data are of value? And is it possible to produce data of no

Fig. 4 U5, *PALM Archive*, screenshot, spring 2019.

value? What interests are written into particular programs? Why do I take part **Fig. 4**?

Conference "Art History and New Media: What's Up?," October 2021, Basel

While presenting past experiments in teaching art history and media theory from within the digital-analog entanglements that shape our contemporary world, I remembered a quote by Natascha Sadr Haghighian: "If I can't disassemble the device, the artist wrote, I can start by taking apart my visual system. The necessary dispersion of my gaze starts by untying it from the image on the screen and shifting at least half an eye outside the frame, examining the edges of the image and the peripheral areas of the screen in order to grapple with the image and look beyond content."[23]

She further proposes that to look at the depth beyond the surface starts with "deliberately looking awry."[24] In a closely related endeavor, we started by remobilizing bodies of students and teachers, inviting diverse voices, exploring complex territories, mixing formats, and changing perspectives, in order to defamiliarize, to welcome irritations, and to allow for unexpected encounters. For the colloquium at the House of Electronic Arts, I invited the artist collective U5 to collaborate. They sent a pink rabbit named Hasi. "Hasi", I asked, "where is the data"?[25]   //

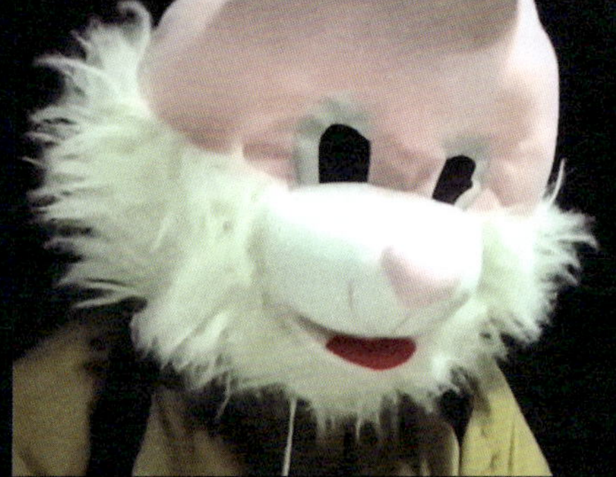

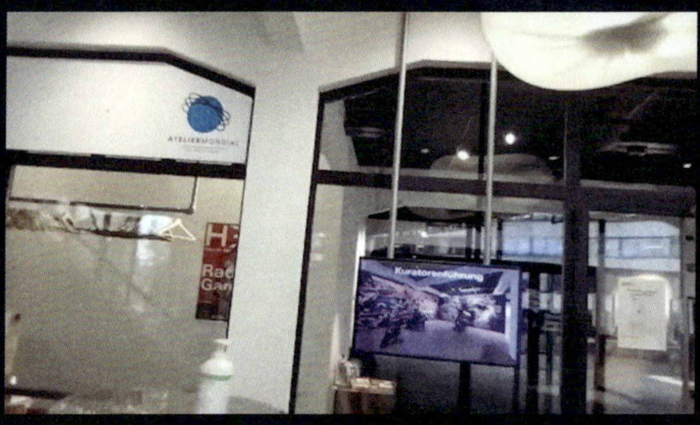

I am looking around. Wait, I want to discover.
Let's go out.
If I would be data, I would be outside.

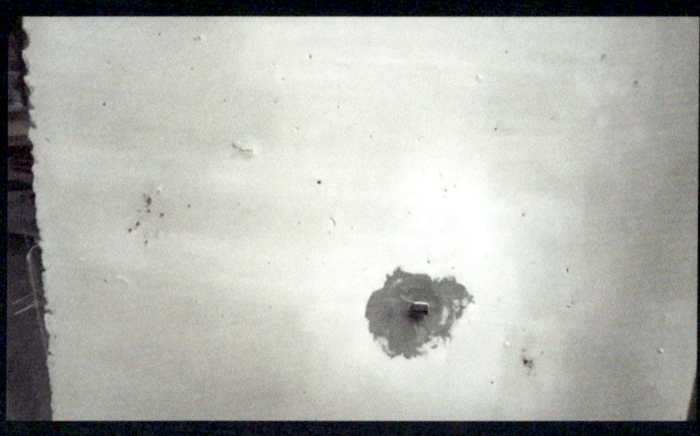

I discovered this. What do you think?
That's data!

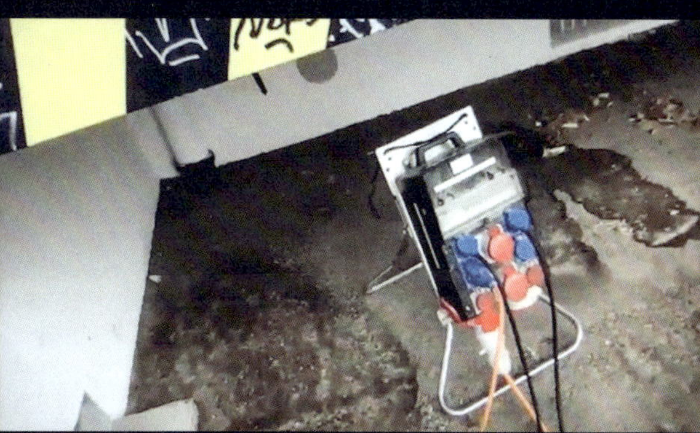

But we want more data!
Here is energy supply, maybe we are close.

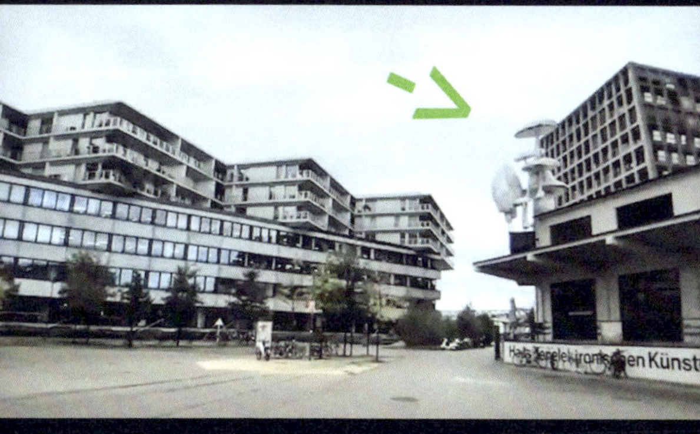

Maybe data is in the sky?
Or in these mushrooms?
Is there some data in the facades of buildings?
Residencial buildings, hidden data, private data

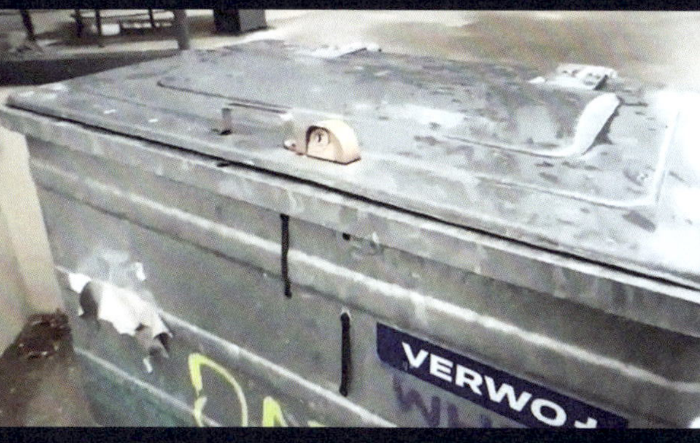

In the trash bin?
You need a key for this data.

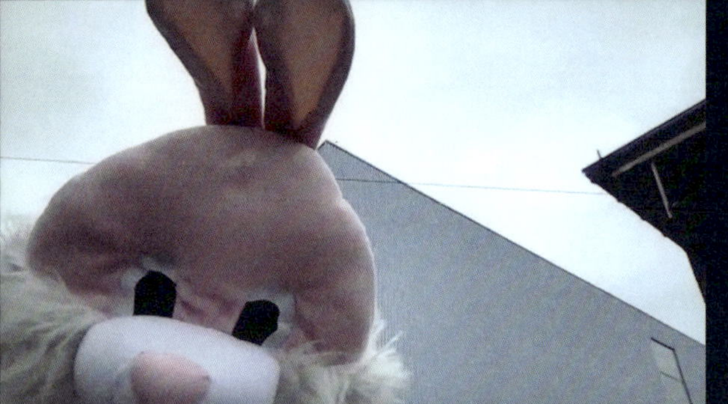

Are you still with me?
Ya, sure!

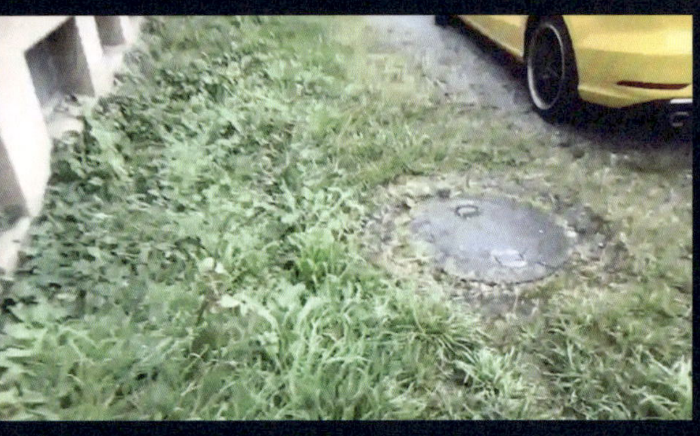

Maybe the plants are hiding all our data?
Are you eating data, Hasi?
Yeah, sometimes, it depends. When I start eating data
I can't stop. I eat so much that I regret eating all

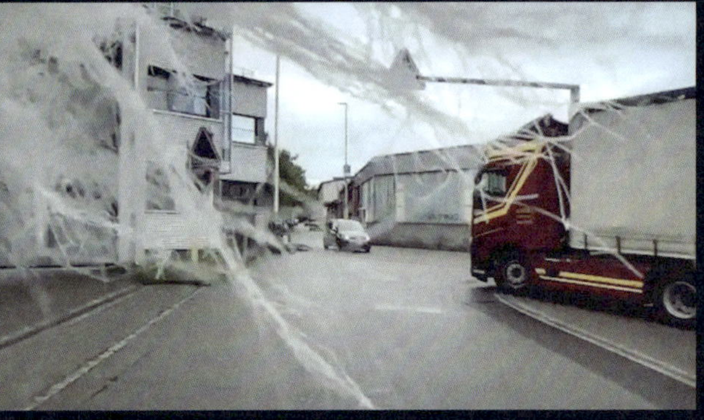

Traffic. Data comes with traffic!
Maybe all the lories transport data?

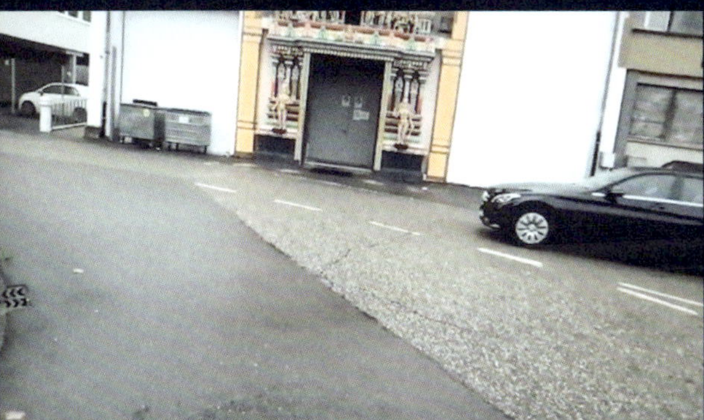

Oh, I discovered some strange data,
in this temple, what do you think?
It's a treasure box!

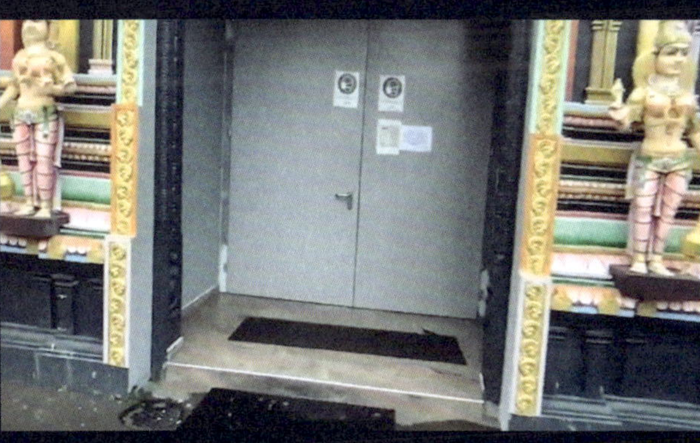

Let's have a look, whether the door is open.

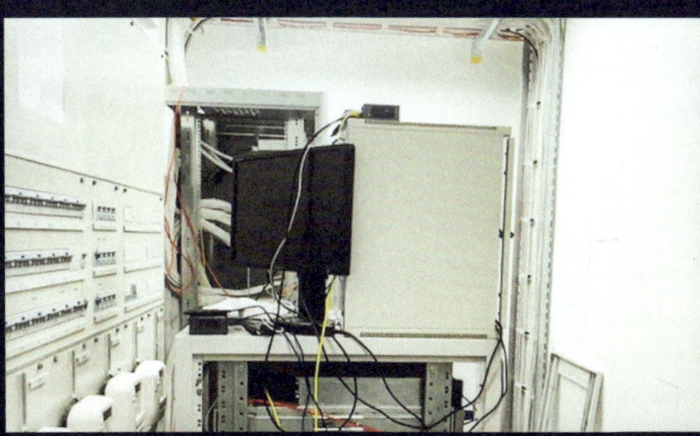

You have found it!

1 For an overview of the series and all related events, please see Rory Pilgrim's website, "Software Garden," accessed November 1, 2022, www.rorypilgrim.com/software-garden/.

2 For political activism around these issues see, e.g., the website of Disabled People Against Cuts (DPAC), accessed March 18, 2023, https://dpac.uk.net.

3 Rory Pilgrim and Human Poney, "The Evolution of Care. A Conversation with Rory Pilgrim on Technology + Activism through the Lens of Spirituality + Joy," AQNB, June 14, 2017, www.aqnb.com/2017/06/14/the-evolution-of-care-a-conversation-with-rory-pilgrim-on-activism-through-the-lens-of-spirituality-and-joy/.

4 Donna Haraway, *Manifestly Haraway* (Minneapolis: University of Minnesota Press, 2016 [1985]), 67.

5 See, e.g., Sardar Ziauddin, "alt.civilizations.faq Cyberspace as the Darker Side of the West," *Futures* 27, no. 7 (September 1995): 777–94; and Shoshana Zuboff, *The Age of Surveillance Capitalism: The Fight for a Human Future at the New Frontier of Power* (New York: PublicAffairs), 2019.

6 Pilgrim and Poney, "The Evolution of Care."

7 "Who is Pepper?," Aldebaran Robotics, accessed May 9, 2023, https://web.archive.org/web/20151006205404/https://www.aldebaran.com/en/a-robots/who-is-pepper/.

8 For one recent example, see Arianna Martinez, "Could Robots Fill the Gaps at Nebraska's Understaffed Senior Living Facilities?," *Nebraska News*, Channel 8 KLKN-TV, September 12, 2022, accessed March 18, 2023, www.klkntv.com/could-robots-fill-the-gaps-at-nebraskas-understaffed-senior-living-facilities/.

9 "Health and Social Care: Developing Robotics and Technologies for Care," Sheffield Robotics, University of Sheffield, accessed March 18, 2023, www.sheffield.ac.uk/sheffieldrobotics/health-and-social-care/.

10 Ursula K. Le Guin, "A Non-Euclidean View of California as a Cold Place to Be" (1982), in *Dancing at the Edge of the World* (London: Gollancz, 1989), 90.

11 Ursula K. Le Guin, "Is Gender Necessary?," in *The Language of the Night: Essays on Fantasy and Science Fiction*, ed. Susan Wood (New York: Putnam, 1979), 163.

12 Donna Haraway, *Staying with the Trouble: Making Kin in the Chthulucene* (Durham, NC: Duke University Press, 2016), 3.

13 Pilgrim and Poney, "The Evolution of Care."

14 Björk, "All Is Full of Love," 1999, music video directed by Chris Cunningham. The song, produced by Howie B, is the tenth track on her album *Homogenic* (1997).

15 The expression "mindless agent" comes from Mireille Hildebrandt, *Smart Technologies and the Ends of Law* (Cheltenham and Northampton, UK: Edward Elgar, 2015), viii.

16 Beatriz Colomina and Mark Wigley, *Are We Human? Notes on an Archaeology of Design* (Zurich: Lars Müller, 2016), 90.

17 This course was titled "Who Cares?," Department of Architecture, ETH Zurich, fall semester 2020, cotaught by Philip Ursprung, Adam Jasper, Tim Klauser, Berit Seidel, and Nina Zschocke.

18 Natascha Sadr Haghighian, "Disco Parallax," in *Relearning Bearing Witness*, ed. Brian Kuan Wood (Berlin and Cologne: n.b.k. and Verlag der Buchhandlung Walther und Franz König, 2021), 127–38.

19 I am borrowing here from Hans-Jörg Rheinberger's characterizations of scientific laboratory practices. See Rheinberger, "Konjunkturen: Transfer-RNA, Messenger-RNA, genetischer Code," in *Objekte Differenzen und Konjunkturen. Experimentalsysteme im historischen Kontext*, ed. Michael Hagner, Hans-Jörg Rheinberger, and Bettina Wahrig-Schmidt (Berlin: Akademie Verlag, 1994), 201–31.

20 This course was titled "Exhibit Inhabit," Department of Architecture, ETH Zurich,

spring semester 2021, cotaught by Philip Ursprung, Adam Jasper, Tim Klauser, Berit Seidel, and Nina Zschocke.

[21] PALM is an acronym for Preview–Archive–Live–Moods. For further information see, PALM platform, accessed March 18, 2023, http://palm.92u.ch.

[22] Nick Srnicek, *Plattform-Kapitalismus* (Hamburg: Hamburger Edition, 2018); Zuboff, *The Age of Surveillance Capitalism*.

[23] Sadr Haghighian, "Disco Parallax," 137.

[24] Sadr Haghighian, "Disco Parallax," 137.

[25] U5 and Nina Zschocke, *Hasi, Where Is the Data?*, 2021, Zoom video, 3:58, © U5.

CREATION, CONSERVATION, MEDIATION

\>\>

06

TRANSLATION OF THE ART AND ARCHITECTURE THESAURUS® IN SWITZERLAND: VISION AND IMPLEMENTATION

Sarah Amsler and Thomas Hänsli

The comprehensive documentation of objects in collections is of crucial significance for museums, collections, and beyond: while it makes the management of an institution's holdings possible, it very often is the only source for museum staff and researchers to contextualize a given object and—where needed—research the object's provenance and the circumstances of how it entered the collection. In recent years, inventories—or parts of them—have regularly appeared online. Cataloging recommendations and rules guiding those in charge of documentation become more important when collections are published online, since they enable the enhancement and interoperability of data between various databases. In addition, documentary language (subject heading lists, classifications, or thesauri) used as metadata is a key element not only as an access point to collections but also for data sharing.

Situation in Switzerland

Although documentary language is widely used in the library field, practices and vocabularies for museum documentation differ greatly from one institution or language region to another. A 2018 survey that the Swiss Art Research Infrastructure (SARI) conducted on the case of cultural, heritage, and research institutions that specialize in art and architecture confirmed such varied practices. Although not representative, this questionnaire-based survey found that, while a few institutions had integrated documentary language of national and international importance as a tool for describing their collections, this mostly pertained to authority records on personal names and corporate bodies as well as locations.[1] For subject indexing, although Iconclass and Trachsler classifications are sometimes used, most entities work with dedicated in-house subject heading lists. Institutions are aware of the disadvantages associated with this choice, particularly concerning the maintenance of these lists and the lack of interoperability between collections that this entails.

These disparities in terms of documentary language probably explain why there are very few portals in Switzerland that compile the collections of various museums; many of these institutions, instead, make their digitized objects available online through their websites or dedicated platforms. The few examples of meta-catalogs available in Switzerland (in most cases, originating from cantonal initiatives or associations) demonstrate that, despite the great qualities of these tools, there is still room for improvement: a search by "subject" does not return the same results in French and German, for example. This reality, which can also be observed in Swiss library environments, highlights the current shortcomings in terms of multilingual subject indexing tools.

There are several reasons for the lack of homogeneity in the use of vocabulary. The major obstacle is certainly multilingualism. Even though Switzerland is considered a multilingual country, institutions often write descriptions in the language of their region. Moreover, as a study conducted in 2019 at the Bern University of Applied Sciences shows, only a minority of repositories and controlled vocabularies are available in the form of linked open data, which does not facilitate their dissemination and reuse.[2]

Art and Architecture Thesaurus®

Among the existing documentary languages, the Art and Architecture Thesaurus® (AAT®) is certainly the most suitable vocabulary for describing objects in art history, architecture, and materials science. While the AAT® is intended for subject indexing, ULAN, TGN, CONA, and IA—the four other vocabularies created, maintained, and made available by the Getty Research Institute—are authority files for names, geographic locations, works of art, objects, and iconography.[3]

Initial work on the AAT®, which was led by the J. Paul Getty Art History Information Program (AHIP) and later by the Getty Research Institute, began in the late 1970s to meet the needs of art libraries and art periodical indexing services and to automate cataloging procedures. Those responsible for the inventory of museum objects and visual resources have subsequently expressed the need to use similar controlled vocabularies to ensure consistency in cataloging and more efficient information retrieval.[4] Initially only available in English, the first edition of the thesaurus contained 17,600 primary terms and 31,000 rejected terms. The 1994 edition contained approximately 25,300 primary terms and 46,000 rejected terms.[5] Thanks to the collaborative approach of the Getty Research Institute, the thesaurus is constantly being enriched with new concepts as well as translations of terms. It currently contains about 56,000 concepts, divided into seven hierarchical facets. Since 2014, the AAT® has also been available in the form of linked open data.

In recent years, several research institutions and museums have carried out translation projects with the aim of making the thesaurus accessible in different languages.[6] Among the major initiatives are the projects of the Netherlands Institute for Art History (RKD) for Dutch (43,936 concepts translated, as of September 2022); the Centro de Documentación de Bienes

Patrimoniales (Servicio Nacional del Patrimonio Cultural, Ministerio de las Culturas, las Artes y el Patrimonio; Santiago, Chile) for Spanish (31,219); the Chinese Academy for the Republic of China (Taiwan) for Chinese (25,347); the Canadian Network for Heritage Information for French (17,198); and the Institut für Museumsforschung (Staatliche Museen zu Berlin, Stiftung Preussischer Kulturbesitz) for German (8,023).

The Missions of the Swiss Art Research Infrastructure (SARI) and the AAT® Translation Project

The Swiss Art Research Infrastructure (SARI), hosted by the University of Zurich, is part of the Swiss Roadmap for Research Infrastructure (2017–20).[7] Its goal is to provide unified and mutual access to research data, collections, digital visual resources, and related reference data in the fields of historical sciences and digital humanities. Documentary language is also integrated in an environment based on semantic web technologies. The AAT® is one of the vocabularies offered by the platform.

Since 2018, SARI has been conducting a project to translate this thesaurus, because the Swiss national languages are not yet sufficiently represented. SARI coordinates the translations at a Swiss level and makes them accessible—that is, usable by humans and machines—to cultural, heritage, and research institutions. The objectives are to make translations of the concepts available in different national languages and in linked open data as well as to encourage a standardization of practices in terms of subject indexing by using a reference documentary language that is widely used internationally.

Given the magnitude of the task—translating all 56,000 concepts into three languages—several strategies have been defined. To date, one-third of the concepts already contain a translation into French, one-seventh into German, and three percent into

Italian. In order to build on the work already undertaken, translators do not retranslate these concepts but instead enrich them by adding Swiss terms. Translations are carried out according to the needs of the institutions within the context of projects and according to defined themes. In addition, the focus is on aligning the AAT® vocabulary with different documentary languages. Depending on the project, SARI is responsible for organizing the translations, advising on editing, validating the quality, providing the infrastructure, and forwarding the results to the Getty Research Institute.

A Platform for this Specific Translation

SARI has developed a special platform to support the entire translation process and to make it accessible. The multilingual context in Switzerland requires different people to translate a single concept. Based on the concepts, "translation containers" are created, each specific to a language. This gives staff members the opportunity to work on the different language versions in parallel and independently. Even if the translators are in charge of the most time-consuming and complex tasks in the process, many people can work together on a translation container. Theplatform manages these separate roles and the access to the containers [Fig. 1]. The work can, therefore, be carried out on the basis of a continuous flow and interactively with all the various protagonists.

Although based on native RDF data provided by the Getty Research Institute, the semantic model has been aligned with standards such as CIDOC-CRM, SKOS, and Ontolex in order to make it compatible with the other models used by SARI and to respond to the specific features of Switzerland's languages. Two elements, in particular, have been adapted: the addition of a category for the indication of lexical variants according to country and the development of gender and number. To ensure broad

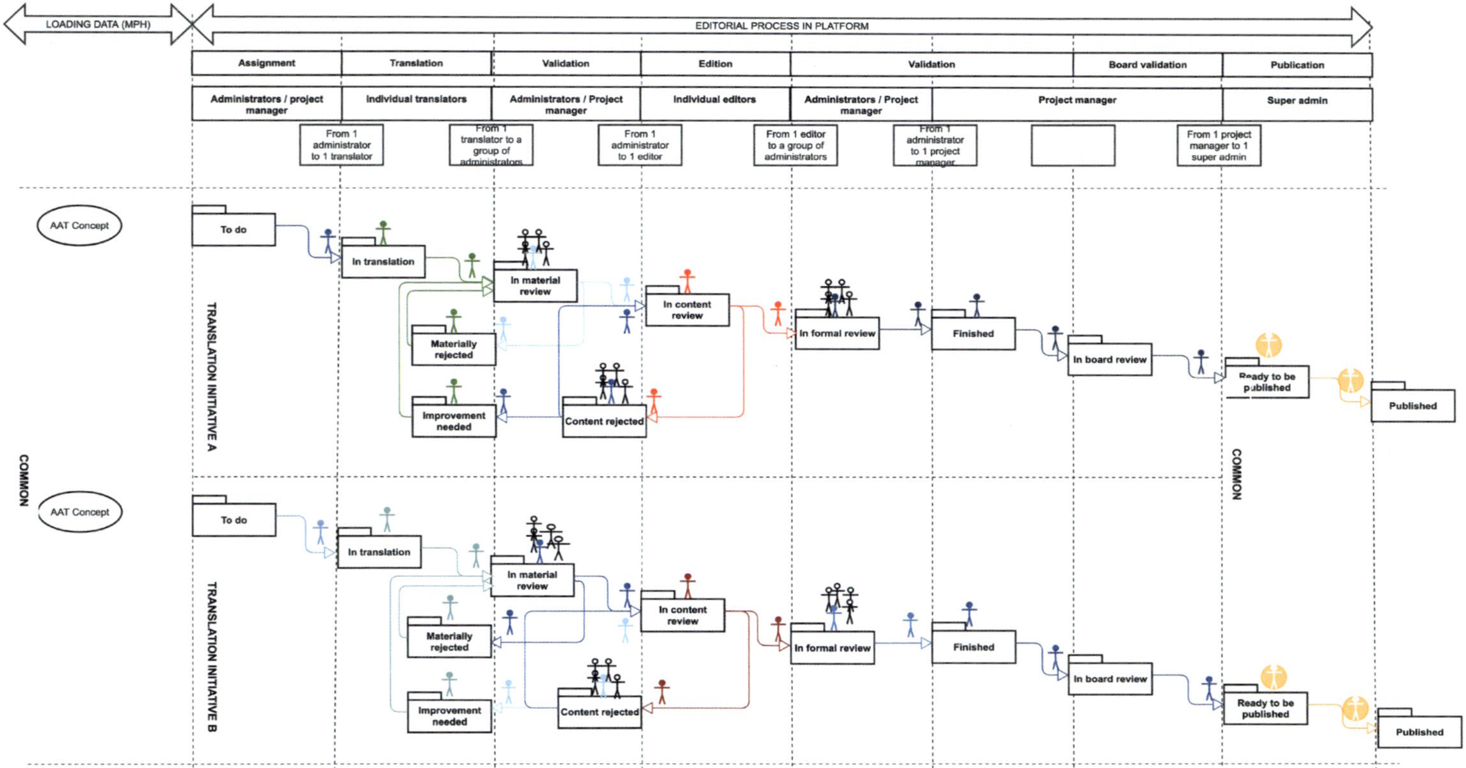

Fig. 1
LOADING DATA (MPH)
EDITORIAL PROCESS IN PLATFORM
Assignment
Translation
Validation
Edition
Validation
Board validation
Publication
Administrators / project manager
Individual translators
Administrators / Project manager
Individual editors
Administrators / Project manager
Project manager
Super admin
From 1 administrator to 1 translator
From 1 translator to a group of administrators
From 1 administrator to 1 editor
From 1 editor to a group of administrators
From 1 administrator to 1 project manager
From 1 project manager to 1 super admin
COMMON
AAT Concept
TRANSLATION INITIATIVE A
To do
In translation
In material review
Materially rejected
Improvement needed
In content review
Content rejected
In formal review
Finished
In board review
Ready to be published
Published
COMMON
AAT Concept
TRANSLATION INITIATIVE B
To do
In translation
In material review
Materially rejected
Improvement needed
In content review
Content rejected
In formal review
Finished
In board review
Ready to be published
Published

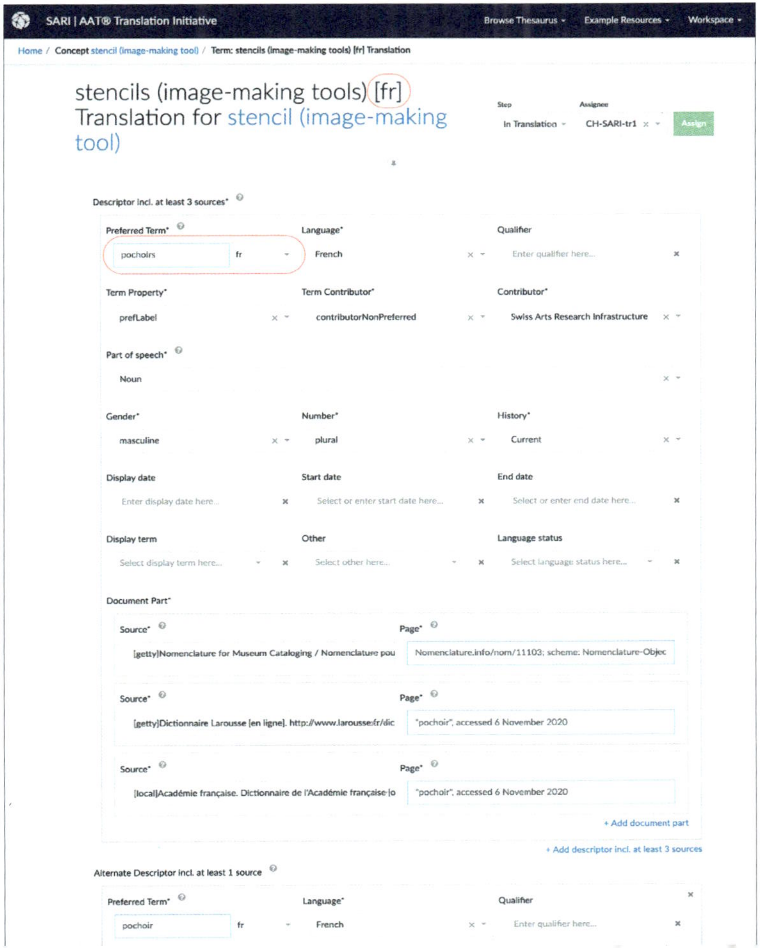

stencils (image-making tools) [fr]
Translation for stencil (image-making tool)

Step: In Translation ▾   Assignee: CH-SARI-tr1 × ▾   **Assign**

Descriptor incl. at least 3 sources*

Preferred Term*: pochoirs | fr ▾   Language*: French × ▾   Qualifier: Enter qualifier here… ×

Term Property*: prefLabel × ▾   Term Contributor*: contributorNonPreferred × ▾   Contributor*: Swiss Arts Research Infrastructure × ▾

Part of speech*: Noun × ▾

Gender*: masculine × ▾   Number*: plural × ▾   History*: Current × ▾

Display date: Enter display date here… ×   Start date: Select or enter start date here… ×   End date: Select or enter end date here… ×

Display term: Select display term here… ▾ ×   Other: Select other here… ▾ ×   Language status: Select language status here… ▾ ×

Document Part*

Source*: [getty]Nomenclature for Museum Cataloging / Nomenclature pou   Page*: Nomenclature.info/nom/11103; scheme: Nomenclature-Objec

Source*: [getty]Dictionnaire Larousse [en ligne]. http://www.larousse.fr/dic   Page*: "pochoir", accessed 6 November 2020

Source*: [local]Académie française. Dictionnaire de l'Académie française [o   Page*: "pochoir", accessed 6 November 2020

+ Add document part

+ Add descriptor incl. at least 3 sources

Alternate Descriptor incl. at least 1 source

Preferred Term*: pochoir | fr ▾   Language*: French × ▾   Qualifier: Enter qualifier here… ×

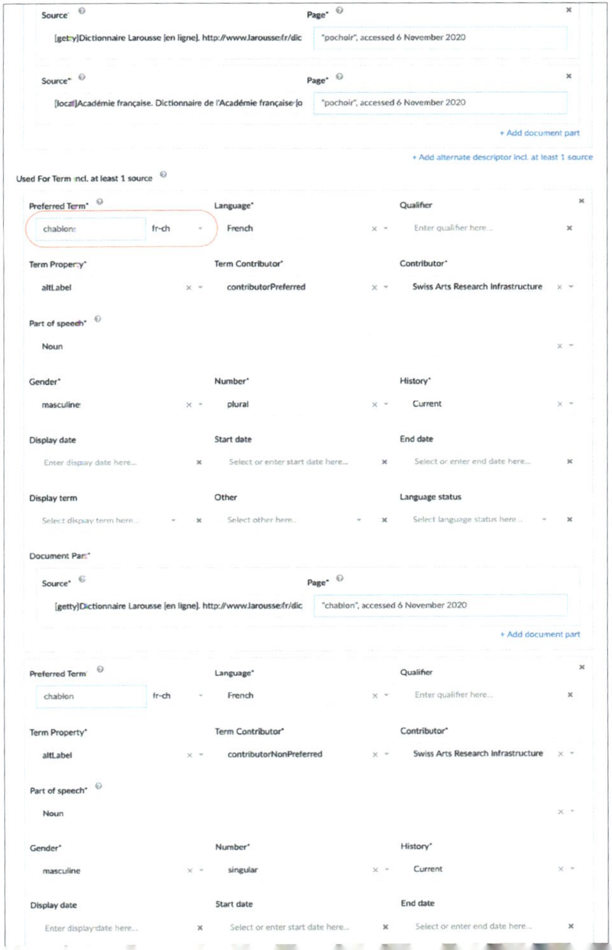

Source*: [getty]Dictionnaire Larousse [en ligne]. http://www.larousse.fr/dic   Page*: "pochoir", accessed 6 November 2020 ×

Source*: [local]Académie française. Dictionnaire de l'Académie française [o   Page*: "pochoir", accessed 6 November 2020 ×

+ Add document part

+ Add alternate descriptor incl. at least 1 source

Used For Term incl. at least 1 source

Preferred Term*: chablons | fr-ch ▾   Language*: French × ▾   Qualifier: Enter qualifier here… ×

Term Property*: altLabel × ▾   Term Contributor*: contributorPreferred × ▾   Contributor*: Swiss Arts Research Infrastructure × ▾

Part of speech*: Noun × ▾

Gender*: masculine × ▾   Number*: plural × ▾   History*: Current × ▾

Display date: Enter display date here… ×   Start date: Select or enter start date here… ×   End date: Select or enter end date here… ×

Display term: Select display term here… ▾ ×   Other: Select other here… ▾ ×   Language status: Select language status here… ▾ ×

Document Part*

Source*: [getty]Dictionnaire Larousse [en ligne]. http://www.larousse.fr/dic   Page*: "chablon", accessed 6 November 2020

+ Add document part

Preferred Term*: chablon | fr-ch ▾   Language*: French × ▾   Qualifier: Enter qualifier here… ×

Term Property*: altLabel × ▾   Term Contributor*: contributorNonPreferred × ▾   Contributor*: Swiss Arts Research Infrastructure × ▾

Part of speech*: Noun × ▾

Gender*: masculine × ▾   Number*: singular × ▾   History*: Current × ▾

Display date: Enter display date here…   Start date: Select or enter start date here…   End date: Select or enter end date here… ×

crm:P73_has_language
<https://glottolog.org/resource/languoid/id/stan1293>
crm:E55_Type
gvp:Subject
skos:Concept
ontolex:LexicalConcept
<sari/12345>
ontolex:lexicalizedSense
ontolex:lexicalizedSense
ontolex:LexicalEntry
<sari/4567/en>
ontolex:LexicalEntry
<sari/12345/de>
ontolex:canonicalForm
skosxl:prefLabel
gvp:termFlag
<http://vocab.getty.edu/term/flag/Vernacular>
dc:identifier
"1000588968"
crm:E39_Actor
foaf:Agent
lexinfo:singular
<sari/term/singular>
lexinfo:number
gvp:contributorPreferred
<sari/term/12345/lex/1/mp>
crm:E33_Linguistic_Object
skosxl:Literal
ontolex:Form
skosxl:prefLabel
ontolex:canonicalForm
"comment about form"@en
rdfs:comment
<sari/12345/de/lex/1/ms>
crm:E33_Linguistic_Object
skosxl:Label
ontolex:Form
gvp:termType
skos:Concept
<http://vocab.getty.edu/term/type/Descriptor>
"flourishing"@en
ontolex:writtenRep
gvp:TermPOS
gvp:estStart
""xsd:date
lexinfo:gender
lexinfo:masculine
<sari/term/masculine>
gvp:termKind
gvp:historicFlag
<http://vocab.getty.edu/historic/current>
gvp:displayOrder
gvp:qualifier
"qualifier"@en
gvp:termDisplay
"1"
gvp:term
skos:Concept
<http://vocab.getty.edu/term/POS/Noun>
<http://vocab.getty.edu/term/display/Display>
skos:Concept
<http://vocab.getty.edu/term/kind/JargonOrSlang>
gvp:sourcePreferred
skosxl:literalForm
"Darsteller"@de
ontolex:writtenRep
crm:E73_Information_Object
bibo:Document
p2 has type
E55 Type
rdfs:label
"citation"
crm:P73_has_language
<https://glottolog.org/resource/languoid/id/stan1295>

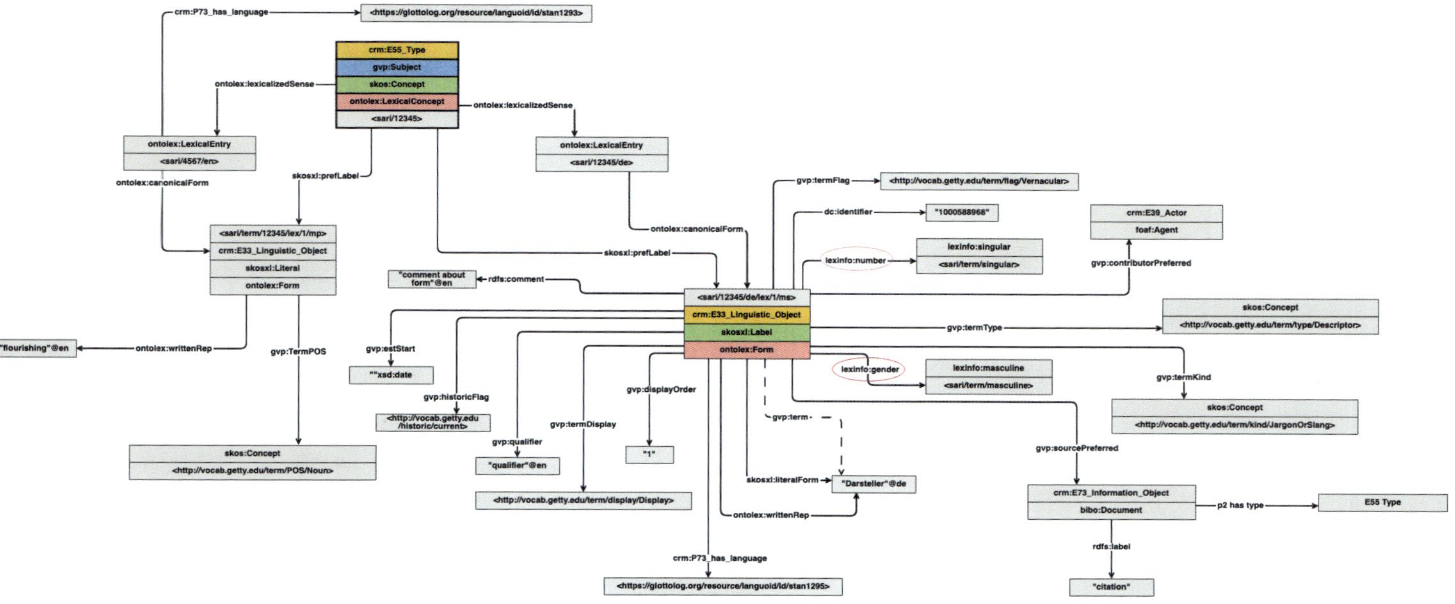

Fig. 3

use of the thesaurus in the description of Swiss collections, regional terms or spelling variants must be included. For instance, while the term *pochoir* is the French translation of the English concept of *stencils*, the term *chablon* is preferred in Switzerland.[8] For the German language, take the example of *Dachboden* and *Estrich* for the concept of attics (interior spaces).[9] The spelling variants are especially frequent because Swiss German systematically replaces the Eszett (*ß*) with two s's (*ss*). The interface, therefore, makes it possible to document these differences in the system **Fig. 2**. Concerning gender and number, it was necessary to model the grammatical categories used by the Getty in more detail. While in the original ontological model there is only one "part of speech" element to indicate the gender, the number, and the grammatical category to which a term belongs, SARI has integrated the Ontolex/Lexinfo ontological standards into its model **Fig. 3**.

Fig. 1 Diagram showing the different steps required to translate a concept and the associated roles. Only the people who need to intervene at a specific stage are able to modify or add data to the concept. (previous page)

Fig. 2 Work form for the introduction of the different terms corresponding to a concept. This example shows that it is perfectly possible to document the various regional specificities and to mention them by means of a code, such as "fr–ch" for Swiss French. (previous page)

Fig. 3 Data model in the translation interface showing the different ontology alignments.

Different Methodological Approaches to Translation

The current translation projects of the AAT® follow several approaches. The choice of entries to be translated can be made from what is already available in the thesaurus. For example, concepts concerning activities or professions have been translated from English into French and German. This selection of concepts corresponds to terms from a list of authority records of persons, which was used in the creation of a platform for the archives of the Institute for the History and Theory of Architecture gta.[10] Another project was carried out in parallel in the field of photography, in which several institutions in Switzerland are specialized. The translations of terminology specific to photography, therefore, satisfy a strong demand from various stakeholders. Since the Biblioteca dell'Accademia di architettura in Mendrisio has already undertaken translations into Italian for the AAT®, the project plans to complete this first step through broader coverage of the topic in different areas of the thesaurus (be it objects, activities, materials, or agents).

A third approach is one adopted for the field of electronic art, which is conducted jointly with the Swiss Institute for Art Research (SIK-ISEA).[11] SIK-ISEA tested its own list of keywords with the concepts available in AAT®. For each of the forty-seven keywords, matches with AAT® are established, and then translations into the three languages are undertaken according to the Getty's guidelines. This will allow the institute to align with the AAT® reference vocabulary and also to validate its own list of subject headings and even to adapt it, if other descriptors should prove to be more appropriate. The translations are carried out by a SIK-ISEA employee specializing in electronic art, and the task is supervised by SARI, particularly in terms of support and quality control.

Conclusion and Perspectives

It is still too early to observe the first integrations of the AAT® as a documentation language into the platforms of museums and research institutions in Switzerland. However, there is interest in this translation project, especially from those in charge of authority records who want to align their vocabularies. More and more heritage, cultural, and scientific institutions are transforming their data into linked open data and, in particular, into the CIDOC-CRM reference model, following the example of the SIK-ISEA research portal and OSCAR.[12] These new developments are very welcome because one of the advantages of linked open data is the greater visibility and availability of that data to a wider community of users. Moreover, once the data have been encoded according to a collaborative standard such as CIDOC-CRM, the data can more easily benefit from SARI's reference data services, which include the Getty vocabularies. The combination of these two methods—data structuring and the use of international documentation language—has the potential to solve the problems of multilingual content and thus open up the data to the rest of the world.

In the specific translation project underway at SARI, there are no plans for all AAT® concepts to be fully translated into the Swiss national languages. A pragmatic solution to achieve this goal would be to integrate AAT® as an indexing vocabulary into existing platforms and to benefit, if available, from the translations resulting from the collaborative work conducted internationally. Gaps could then be identified and targeted for translation. In addition, in a system that supports linked open data, the AAT® concept could be displayed according to the language used to connect to the platform. If a concept is later enriched with a new term, this term would be automatically displayed in the interface. It is also possible to display the terms in languages other than French, German, Italian, and English and thus to highlight, through subject indexing, Swiss heritage collections beyond the national territory.

It should be noted that the AAT® is not just suitable for describing museum collections or research data. Indeed, the origin of this vocabulary is in the library community for subject cataloging. For heritage, cultural, and research institutions specializing in the history of art and related fields, the prospect of using a single documentary language, regardless of the medium described (book, image, work of art, archive), not only would help staff to develop professional skills for a single indexing vocabulary but, above all, would offer homogeneity in terms of access to the various collections held or studied.   //

1 See, e.g., the "Gemeinsame Normdatei (GND)," accessed March 18, 2023, https://explore.gnd.network/, and "Rameau," accessed March 18, 2023, https://catalogue.bnf.fr/recherche-autorite.do?pageRech=rat/; SIKART *Lexicon on art in Switzerland*, accessed March 18, 2023, www.sikart.ch; and the *Dictionnaire historique de la Suisse*, accessed March 18, 2023, https://hlsdhs-dss.ch. For an example of records on locations, see "GeoNames," accessed March 18, 2023, www.geonames.org.

2 Beat Estermann et al., *Basisregister und kontrollierte Vokabulare als Wegbereiter für Linked Open Data in der Schweiz. Innovationsprojekt von E-Government-Schweiz im Auftrag des Schweizerischen Bundesarchivs* (Bern: Berner Fachhochschule, Institut Public Sector Transformation, 2020), 29.

3 See "Union List of Artist Names®," accessed March 18, 2023, www.getty.edu/research/tools/vocabularies/ulan/; "Getty Thesaurus of Geographic Names®", accessed March 18, 2023, www.getty.edu/research/tools/vocabularies/tgn/; and "Cultural Objects Name Authority®" and "Getty Iconography Authority™," accessed March 18, 2023, www.getty.edu/research/tools/vocabularies/cona/. See also Anne Helmreich and Patricia Harpring, "Digital Art History and the Getty Vocabularies" (PowerPoint presentation, 108th CAA Annual Conference, Chicago, IL, 2020), accessed March 18, 2023, www.getty.edu/research/tools/vocabularies/CAA_Getty_Vocabs_workshop.pdf.

4 "History of the AAT," website of the Getty Research Institute, accessed March 18, 2023, www.getty.edu/research/tools/vocabularies/aat/about.html#history/.

5 Pat Molholt and Toni Petersen, "The Role of the 'Art and Architecture Thesaurus' in Communicating About Visual Art," *Knowledge Organization* 20, no. 1 (1993): 30–34.

6 Murtha Baca, "Multilingual AAT and Digital Art History Work at the Academia Sinica," *Visual Resources* 29, no. 4 (2013): 273–75; Winfried Bergmeyer, "Die deutsche Fassung des Art & Architecture Thesaurus," *AKMB-news* 20, no. 2 (2014): 13–15; Lina Nagel and Chris Miller, "The Tesauro de Arte & Arquitectura and Tesauro Regional Patrimonial: Tools for Describing and Enhancing Access to Latin American Cultural Resources Online," *Getty Research Journal*, no. 5, (2013): 149–56.

7 See the Federal Council's press release "2015 Research Infrastructures Roadmap," State Secretariat for Education, research and Innovation SERI, Swiss Confederation, posted June 24, 2015, www.admin.ch/gov/en/start/documentation/media-releases.msg-id-57808.html.

8 AAT®, s.v. "stencils (image-making tools)," accessed March 18, 2023, http://vocab.getty.edu/page/aat/300022777/.

9 AAT®, s.v. "attics (interior spaces)," accessed March 18, 2023, http://vocab.getty.edu/page/aat/300004076/.

10 The project involves making the data from the archival holdings and digitized visual resources of the archive of the Institute for the History and Theory of Architecture gta, at ETH Zurich, as well as data from related research projects, accessible through a research portal. See "gta Research Portal," website of SARI, accessed March 18, 2023, http://swissartresearch.net/portfolio/gta-research-portal/.

11 SIK-ISEA is one of SARI's official partners. See the website of SIK-ISEA, accessed March 18, 2023, www.sik-isea.ch.

12 See Matthias Oberli, "Das Schweizerische Institut für Kunstwissenschaft (SIK-ISEA) und die kunsthistorische Grundlagenforschung im digitalen Zeitalter," *Zeitschrift für Schweizerische Archäologie und Kunstgeschichte (ZAK)* 77, nos. 2–3 (2020): 129, 135; and Christian Weiss, "Das Online Swiss

Coin Archive (OSCAR)—Numismatik und Normdaten im Schweizerischen National-museum," *Zeitschrift für Schweizerische Archäologie und Kunstgeschichte (ZAK)* 77, nos. 2–3 (2020): 185–92.

#07

THE "RETOUR AUX SOURCES" RESEARCH PROJECT: HOW TO THINK AND PRACTICE DIGITAL CREATION IN FRENCH ART SCHOOLS

Keyvane Alinaghi and Caroline Tron-Carroz

This article stems from the "Retour aux Sources" (Back to the sources) research project that was launched in 2019 at the Ecole Supérieure d'Art et de Communication de Cambrai (ESAC) in France.[1] Similar to many art-school projects, the "Retour aux Sources" (RAS) project has evolved in a palpably digital environment, which is dependent on the resources exchanged every day on the Internet or other networks. This exchange is stimulated by the open-source spirit that has been present in contemporary art and culture since the 1970s.[2] Art history has expanded its field under the influence of digital culture, coming to include media archaeology, digital humanities, and the maker movement, bringing a new approach to past and present technological and digital creations.[3] Looking at how new technologies and their uses are developed and shared today is also a way of questioning the kind of digital culture in which art-school students are involved. How do they think and practice collectively as part of such an endeavor? How do they claim an open, unstandardized graphic design by initiating a creation based on day-by-day exploration? Furthermore, we might ask what are the theoretical and technical tools that help us to think about digital creation in French art schools? And finally, how can we free ourselves from industrial software and its hermetic, redundant formats that constrain creativity? These are some of the major questions addressed by RAS. We suggest some pathways of analysis in this essay.

The article aims primarily to present the scientific intentions and selected case studies from the RAS research project about how art schools safeguard and accord value to digital creations in the general context of sharing and perpetuating devices and challenging planned obsolescence, unregulated content, and preconceived creation environments in the many subfields of graphic design and the contemporary digital arts.

Artistic Heritage

For several decades, the Ecole Supérieure d'Art et de Communication de Cambrai (ESAC) has encouraged digital practices with the use of locked tools, such as the Adobe suite. This practice contradicts one of the baselines of digital creation in a pedagogical environment, where the machine is intended as a tool for emancipation and not one of confinement. At the beginning of office computing, in the 1970s, the personal computer (PC) was thought of as an instrument to be built, experimented with, and developed using lines of code and software. The computer has, therefore, become increasingly self-enclosed, providing ready-to-use tools with preinstalled applications.[4] This question of the technological tool restricting practice runs through the entire art history of objects with technological components. Each generation of artists has displaced the technical medium to rethink the social forms of its use. Many avant-garde and post-avant-garde artists have shared the idea that art is a factor of social and technical deconditioning. And, through various examples, drawn especially from the field of analog or predigital art, educators show their students how artists have always invited us to see electronic devices, such as the television set, differently, to liberate images trapped in a rigid format. Indeed, many experimental electronic works have rethought routine behaviors, visual habits, and repetitive gestures in front of screens.

The RAS research program is deeply rooted in the history of electronic and video art. For instance, in the early 1960s, Nam June Paik began to work with the cathode-ray-tube television, which became a very malleable artistic medium. The artist increased the vibratory aspect of the electronic image and developed abstract images with the light signal, distortions, or lines to think about the electronic potentialities of the television set. Today, the computer is also seen as a field of art experimentation in the face of industry or marketing discourse, which defends the culture of the disposable to the detriment of innovation. The knowledge (code and history of the medium) transmitted at ESAC aims to make students autonomous in their creations in order to facilitate understanding of a digital artwork. Following the example of reverse engineering techniques in the hard sciences, the Ateliers de Recherche et de Création (ARC) invited participants to break down and recompose digital works to understand how they function. The workshops also prompted dialogue with older tools, such as monitors, oscilloscopes, and Minitels, by transposing the computer code onto the analog medium. Learning to create with existing materials shows students the possible flows and connections between analog and digital media, guiding them toward an existing open creation. Indeed, another way of being innovative is to not consider the media heritage of the twentieth century as an obsolete resource and to instead view it as an operational resource compatible with contemporary digital creation.

The RAS project charts ways in which artists have quickly changed the logic of device use. It also argues against the formatting of minds and tools as in Nam June Paik's involvement in the series *Robots* (1980s). The *Robots* are representations of artificial intelligence: they are immobile, unarticulated, and unconnected. Yet, through this series of video sculptures, the artist develops a strategy, admittedly elementary, for countering the planned obsolescence that marks the history of analog creations. In this case, Paik has replaced vintage equipment with new material. This diversion of objects is in line with the practices of his greatest artistic inspirations, Marcel Duchamp and John Cage, but even more so with the philosophy of Fluxus, which consists, among other things, of producing infinite potentialities between artists and technological objects. Therefore, it is crucial to convey to students that Paik is one of those artists who opposes outdated technologies and has invented their own tools to work with the electronic image and communicate it to everyone.[5]

Using Existing or Obsolete Material to Create and Preserve

These historical experimentations are essential in raising students' awareness of the unreasoned determinism of planned obsolescence in their creations. An art historical approach facilitates the disclosure of a whole ecosystem of defined, locked, and disposable material. In this respect, the most relevant historical examples are those that imply an error and reverse the plug-and-play logic, thereby demonstrating that media are subject to different social, cultural, and technical practices. The hands-on laboratory approach of the RAS project has prompted a philosophy of historical permeability between analog and digital art. Indeed, this is the very meaning of "back" (*retour*) to the sources.

The notion of historical permeability also includes digital conservation, as can be seen in the attention paid by artists Claire Williams, Antonin Fourneau, Botborg, and Niklas Roys to the diversion and recycling of electronic materials. This self-organized aesthetic practice echoes institutional approaches to the valuing of digital art. The art exists online, where the constant evolution of languages and forms challenges the faithful presentation of pioneering technology-based works. Museums such as the ZKM | Center for Art and Media Karlsruhe approach this question through emulation, whereas other works are stored on outdated CD-ROMs or described in art books.

But these modes of transmission lose the very essence of digital art or graphics—namely, interactivity. Moreover, the updating of digital works is eminently problematic insofar as it affects the integrity of the original work, its safeguarding, and its conservation. This situation and the initiatives envisaged concerning the conservation of digital works as a form of heritage open up a virtual space for reflection on how to preserve analog creations and the challenges of their replacement.[6] In RAS, we considered whether an art school could be a suitable place to think about how to preserve and value digital creations (net art, artistic applications, dynamic images, etc.) and what the conditions would be for preserving a work through programming instead of through its medium. Unlike the work of digital art conservators, our students' creations do not involve "remodeling," nor do they consider the devices' degrees of "reparability." Thus, our methods of reactivating digital works use computer code, not emulation. In addition, it is essential to remind students of the history of the counterculture, to encourage them to see and hear the artists who have created counter-places to the dominant media, such as the Californian "Flower Hackers" and the culture of making.[7] In the early 1970s, when the Internet was still just a prospective idea, artists and computer amateurs were already dealing with electronic information networks and deconstructing centralized mass media logic. A valuable example can be seen in the work of the Ant Farm video collective (Doug Michels, Chip Lord, and Curtis Schreier).

Ant Farm initially sought out innovative and alternative spaces, such as inflatable structures, advocating nomadism against the backdrop of the dominant sedentary model. The collective very quickly used video to produce images for networked sharing communities (*Trukstop Network*, 1975). The theoretical part of the video periodical *Radical Software* is also relevant, since this was one of the conduits of the alternative, anti-television spirit, with texts by artists, philosophers, and thinkers all interested in technology and in computing as a means of emancipation.[8] *Radical Software* was cofounded in 1970 by two women, Beryl Korot and Phyllis Gershuny, which speaks to the role of women across video and computer practices.[9]

These US examples are an integral part of the first case studies included on European and international (art) media history, as some of the contributions in this publication suggest. This artistic heritage mainly shows that critical tools opposing passive techniques and technologies create different reference points that benefit the emancipation of art students.

Reverse Engineering as a Method for Innovation in Art Schools

Following the Bologna Process, French art schools have developed a specific research methodology for graduate studies. This methodology mixes theoretical exploration and artistic experimentation. In artistic creation, it encourages practical engagement by requiring the use of mixed media, tools, devices, and techniques that are related both to art schools' field research and to the digital sphere.[10]

As discussed above, workshops and artistic disciplines are increasingly moving toward the digital realm. Our world is becoming computerized, and new technologies are redefining our societies, our economy, and our modes of communication and representation. Artists and designers are no longer simply creators of content; they also produce the relational interfaces that link human beings and machines. Most often, designers are involved at the end of the technology chain and have to deal with hermetic algorithms and devices regarded as black boxes. Even if this approach does not require the same skills as those of a computer engineer, it is nevertheless essential for designers to understand how a code is structured to know and thus facilitate the use of digital devices.

Similarly, like any artistic work, pieces related to new technologies require writing that, in this case, is inherently linked to digital devices and computer programming. This raises the question of how code is taught in art schools and assimilated into students' work. Within a few years, teaching solutions (empirical methods, hacking), software (Pure Data, Processing, p5.js), and hardware (Arduino), originating in various communities of artists and developers, have managed to define another pathway to technical innovation by opening up digital practices and popularizing computer code. Like media labs, art schools seem to be suitably interdisciplinary laboratories in which students and a heterogeneous teaching team can investigate the methodologies of making new technologies and think about our relationship with the digital world.

Because of their governance and pedagogical autonomy, French art schools enjoy a high degree of freedom of thought and action, which encourages them to deviate from the tech giants' disruptive model.[11] Without the pressures of financial goals, viral marketing, the culture of performance, and the "siliconization" of the world largely kept at bay, art students aim to develop forms of digital design that are ethical and adaptable to a controversial social and ecological environment.[12]

One of the aims of RAS is to transpose real-time culture into a long-term existence by revising or adapting old devices with current technologies to create objects that can stand outside of time. How can we teach interactive design when the historical works presented as references are no longer visible or usable? How can we select essential pieces of interactive design and understand their aesthetic and functional impact on our digital uses by deconstructing them theoretically and by trying to reprogram them through perennial algorithmic tools? Beyond this reverse-engineering exercise, the bringing together of current programming techniques and former digital creations has sparked an interest, particularly among students who are digital natives, in outdated or abandoned concepts that are now gaining a second life thanks to the trends of upcycling, low tech, and digital sobriety, which have emerged against the backdrop of the major challenges posed by the ecological transition.

Creative Coding Workshops: Alternative Proposals to Current Digital Uses

In 2021, students from ESAC questioned the representation of their work published online and the possible alternatives to mainstream social networks by using open-source methods. One of the main problems of the social web is the lack of civic-mindedness and reasoned communication. By using several documentation methods, students discovered the first switched networks and the birth of Internet Relay Chat (IRC), which is regulated by an informal social contract: netiquette.[13] This contract defined the rules of good behavior and politeness on these first participative platforms and introduced the moderation of comments. The revelation of a benevolent social web, self-regulated by a series of tacit rules, led students to identify the turning point that disrupted these spaces of ordered discussion in favor of social networks comprising narcissistic content and anarchic regulation.[14] One of the hypotheses put forward is the shift from detailed forum interfaces to a radical display of simple media (photos and short videos replace long texts),

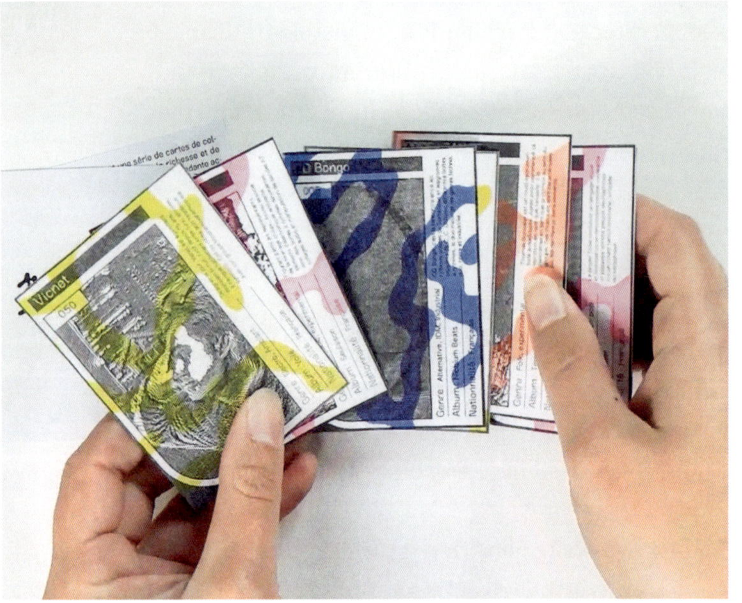

Fig. 1

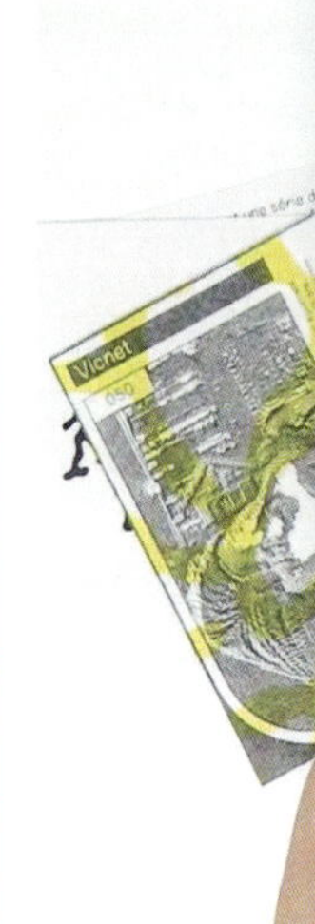

Fig. 2

which are classified by the popular evaluation of the individual Internet user ("subscribe" or "like" buttons).

On the basis of these observations, the student team, named "Silicone Cambrai," worked on the construction of an open-source forum that was not subject to the dictatorship of likes and followers and that had chronologically classified content, regulated by a charter of good conduct. The objective was to build a self-managed platform open to students from other art schools to communicate about their work, discuss freely, and organize professional meetings. The low-tech site (skyblox. org) is composed of a framework reminiscent of the first web forums and follows contemporary aesthetic rules to achieve better energy saving on both the client and server sides.[15] Online since February 8, 2022, the website transforms and updates itself according to the skills acquired by the students.

Another experience that reflects temporal transpositions in the history of new technologies is the overconsumption of

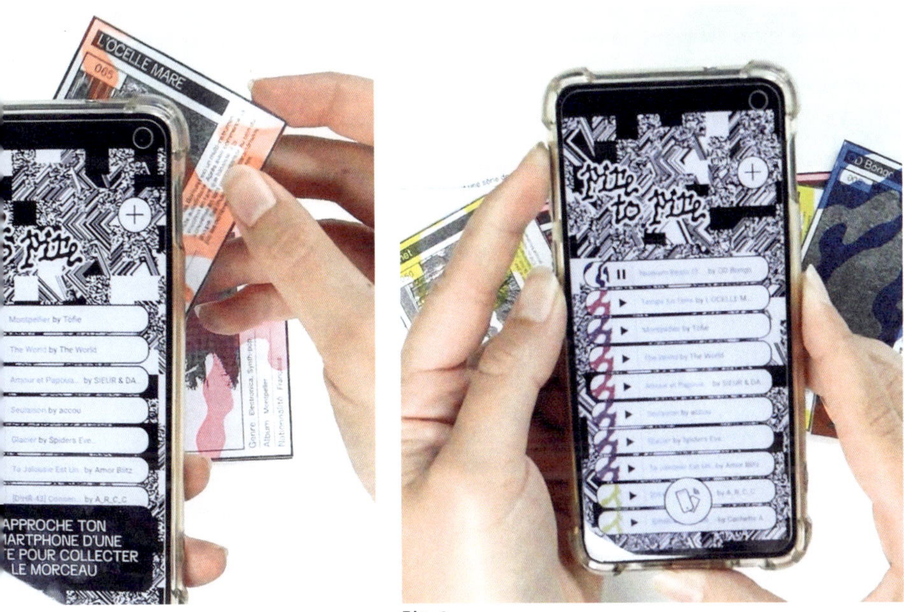

Fig. 3

streaming content and its impact on our carbon footprint.[16] In the field of music, new playback features (the infinite playlist and automated recommendations) lead to overconsumption and encourage an intensified production of new sound compositions. With an awareness of these harmful digital practices, the student researchers deployed the same investigative methods to find rational, yet neglected digital practices, and they are trying to update them. The peer-to-peer principle and direct exchanges of resources between computers (managed by software such as Napster, Soulseek, etc.) have been adapted to create a collectible card game called Pire to Pire, which consists of seven-card packs documenting musicians represented by independent French labels.[17] Each card contains an NFC chip that, when scanned by a cell phone, activates an application and adds the musician's significant album to an audio player [Figs. 1, 2, 3]. The intention is to set up the catalog for each label on the basis of

Fig. 1 Pire to Pire, 7-cards packs, 2022.

Fig. 2 Pire to Pire, NFC chip scanned by a cell phone, 2022.

Fig. 3 Pire to Pire, application, 2022.

a tangible peer-to-peer protocol and to encourage dialogue, the meeting of users, and the exchanging of cards. The DNA of the RAS project is rooted in a reflexive practice of computer coding and in the legacy of digital knowledge.

Moreover, by contributing to the RAS project website, each class of students passes the baton on to the next while also disseminating information to other art schools. This transmission mode relies on theoretical and practical knowledge, encouraging students to reflect collectively on the role of the digital in learning and, more generally, in the society in which they live. These two experiments, selected from other RAS projects, illustrate the need for our art and design students to question the relevance of our use of new technologies. Confrontation of their digital behaviors concerning obsolete devices leads to the resurrection of those objects in better formulations and in more relevant hybrid set-ups that comply with the latest recommendations of the ecological transition while simultaneously preserving the sophisticated and most efficient qualities of current digital technologies. //

[1] Until 2024, the research project "Retour aux sources: La création numérique reconsidérée" (RAS) (Back to the sources: Reconsidering digital creation) is funded by the Direction Générale de la Création Artistique (DGCA) of the French Ministry of Culture. See the project website, http://ras.esac-cambrai.net. On similar issues, "Preservation & Art—Media Archaeology Lab" (PAMAL), Avignon School of Art (ESAA), has been a pioneer in French art schools (2013–19).

[2] Camille Bosqué, *Open Design. Fabrication numérique et mouvement maker* (Paris: Editions B42, 2021).

[3] Anthony Masure, *Design et humanités numériques* (Paris: Editions B42, 2017).

[4] In the 1990s, in France, this choice contributed to the democratization of computers at a time when the French national education system did not yet include computer training.

[5] Paik made the *Paik-Abe Video Synthesizer* (1969–72) together with engineer Shuya Abe without complying with the exclusivity clause.

[6] Ben Fino-Radin, "Conversation in Collections of Digital Works of Art," *The Electronic Media Review* 2 (2021): 101–12.

[7] See Fred Turner, *From Counterculture to Cyberculture: Stewart Brand, the Whole Earth Network and the Rise of Digital Utopianism* (Chicago: University of Chicago Press, 2006).

[8] See the website of *Radical Software*, accessed March 10, 2023, www.radicalsoftware.org/e/index.html. See also the website for the 2018 ZKM exhibition "Radical Software: The Raindance Foundation, for Media Ecology and Video Art," accessed March 10, 2023, https://zkm.de/en/exhibition/2018/06/radical-software/.

[9] *Computer GRrrrls. Histoire.s, genre.s, technologie.s*, exhibition at Hartware MedienKunstVerein (HMKV), Dortmund, Germany, and Gaîté Lyrique, Paris, 2019, curated by Inke Arns and Marie Lechner.

[10] Samuel Bianchini, ed., *Recherche & Création. Art, technologie, pédagogie, innovation* (Nancy: Ecole Nationale Supérieure d'Architecture, Les Éditions du Parc and Montrouge: Burozoïque, 2009), 23.

[11] Philippe Delmas, *Un pouvoir implacable et doux. La Tech ou l'efficacité pour seule valeur* (Paris: Fayard, 2019), 31–45.

[12] See Eric Sadin, *La Silicolonisation du monde. L'irrésistible expansion du libéralisme numérique* (Paris: L'Echappée, 2016).

[13] Since 2019, ESAC has partnered with the Institut National de l'Audiovisuel (INA) and made available a collection of more than seventy years of French audiovisual archives that can be consulted on their website. In 2021, students from RAS chose the keyword *Internet* to understand the context of this network's creation. The second keyword was *cybernetics*. The result of this documentary research is a fictional work on a poster enhanced with a web app; see https://esac.go.yj.fr/athenea/.

[14] See Eric Sadin, *L'ère de l'individu tyran. La fin d'un monde commun* (Paris: Grasset, 2020), 180–91.

[15] See, in particular, Sarah Garcin's documentation on methods to reduce the energy consumption of a website, "Un site web frugal," accessed March 10, 2023, http://site.sarahgarcin.com/web-frugal/.

[16] Ellen Peirson-Hagger and Katharine Swindells, "How Environmentally Damaging Is Music Streaming?," *New Statesman*, November 5, 2021, www.newstatesman.com/environment/2021/11/how-environmentally-damaging-is-music-streaming/.

[17] The pun, "pire to pire," in the game's name can be translated as "worse to worse."

08

NEW MEDIA FOR THE VISUALIZATION OF ARCHITECTURE

Dominik Lengyel and Catherine Toulouse

New Media in Architecture

New media have completely taken over architecture in the last twenty years.[1] In the field of architecture, no media ever seem new anymore; the formerly new media have become essential to the entire chain, from creation to implementation. Sometimes it might be desirable if the much-hyped connection between the head and the hand in drawing were more frequently reactivated to prevent it appearing as if the dissatisfactory evolution of new media were responsible for any unexpected or undesirable results. New media have long since lost their novelty in architecture. The question of what advantages they offer—and even whether they offer such advantages—over the predigital way of creating is unlikely to play any role because of new media's seemingly inevitable use.

Special significance is assigned to the somewhat vague but generic development called *artificial intelligence,* which is becoming increasingly important in the humanities but is used differently in architecture. Whereas in the humanities artificial intelligence above all involves the identification of unexpected connections resulting, for example, from a comprehensive view of vast historical evidence that can no longer be grasped by the human mind, in architecture artificial intelligence appears attractive simply because of the desire for increased or vicarious creativity. Recent developments such as the generation of photorealistic renderings (at least at first glance) by merely entering keywords serve the almost epic fear of the blank page—that is, of creative perplexity when faced with approaches to a lacking design process.[2]

In this context, new media offer a wealth of possibilities that, when used critically, constitute an invaluable asset, whether in architecture as a field of construction or in collaboration between architecture and the humanities. This occurs when the use of new media in the field of design is deliberate and controlled—for example, when designing forms that symbolize humanities-related content, one provides them with visual expression and, in this way, returns them to the humanities in the form of visible reflections.

Abstraction

The key to accessing humanities-related content lies in abstraction. This term, *abstraction*, can be misleading if the Latin verb *abstrahere* is literally translated as "to pull away." This verb suggests that what is left—that is, the "abstract"—previously existed in an unchanged form, albeit hidden. By contrast, the common meaning of *abstraction* as a "strong simplification" comes much closer to the intended goal here, since it involves generating—for instance, through active design—forms that stand for something not present in physical reality in its current state.[3] This type of abstraction is used in completely different ways, depending on the medium.[4]

Abstraction is omnipresent in language. Language is abstract in itself, but the issue here is the fluency with which little-specified terms are used in everyday speech, without it being customary to question their use. The striking abstraction in terms such as *house* becomes apparent only when asking what kind of house we are talking about or what it might look like. It is not as though such questions would never be asked, but the point is that the term *house* is so common as to never seem inappropriate.

Even in visual abstraction, which is somewhat familiar through the everyday use of symbols, signs, or pictograms, the question of the degree of abstraction rarely arises. Not only are arrows, for example, learned and accepted as symbols of directional signs, but pictograms, such as of strongly abstracted single-story buildings with gable roofs, have become established in everyday use, most recently with the ubiquitous digital "home" button.

In spatial, sculpted abstraction, things are very different. Although wooden toys have long conveyed the same idea of a house as the "home" button, this is about as far as it goes in everyday practice. Outside of architecture, spatial formal abstraction is still most likely to be associated with the fine arts and only rarely with the sciences. Yet, abstraction in a spatial model accomplishes exactly the same thing as in pictures and language—namely, the transmission of a certain idea, such as that of a house, and it essentially does so without further features being named or defined. Only at first glance do these missing features have anything to do with the House without Qualities by Oswald Mathias Ungers—after all, this work involved the construction of a concrete building that embodied the idea of abstraction.[5] Abstract model building, on the other hand, is about conveying an idea that either, as in the case of an architectural project, cannot yet be concretized or, as in the case of humanities hypotheses, may never be. In archaeology, for example, test excavations can confirm that there are no finds in the ground of a particular site and thus help exclude the possibility that traces or fragments still exist.

Mediation

Pictures are useful, not only for illustration purposes but also for further research, in the mediation of abstract content that cannot be embodied by a real object but that refers to an object that cannot yet or can no longer be reconstructed. Similar to the connection between the head and hand in the act of drawing, the translation of hypotheses from word to image is made in such a way as to intensify the exploration of the object on both sides. The concretization of what is said in the visual realm initiates a thought process that, without this stimulus, often occurs later or not at all. Perhaps the most important method used in the architectural design process is to put ideas and thoughts down on paper as directly as possible, not merely to fix them but to reflect on them in the truest sense of the word and to look at them from the outside in order to understand them more deeply.

If, however, these representations are virtual or digital models, then these projections of a spatial model enable not only a visual mediation of the hypothesis but also its spatial verification. This aspect is not insignificant, especially from a scientific point of view, since hypotheses about spatial matters usually refer to a physical reality—that is, they are subject to its laws, such as statics, which already limit their possible compositions. This can result in unexpected or even surprising possibilities, such as the analysis of gaze relations, a related field of study.

Research Contribution and Catalytic Function

In the translation of word to image, unexpected new questions always arise, despite targeted problem definition and careful experimental design; this also occurs in the humanities. Discovering these questions represents the true scientific contribution of visualization and design and not merely the illustration of previously known questions. However, new questions arise on both sides—image and word—through the reflexive effect of the pictorial translation of verbal hypotheses. In terms of the field of architecture, the insight gained relates to the examination of hypothetical spatial concepts, both as an intellectual exercise in dealing with uncertainty in knowledge and as a deeper engagement with historical architecture, which can only unfold its conceptual clarity in the form of the idea, free from traces of wear, weathering, and destruction—those influencing factors that are solely historical and often overlay or even conceal the architectural core, the design idea. The term *ruin romanticism* reflects this distinction between idea and current appearance particularly clearly, since, for example, a fortress at the time of its construction was usually a military building technologically at the height of its time and thus far removed from being a romantic building.

Method

The method for translating design hypotheses into visual artifacts is borrowed from two complementary and mutually interacting subdisciplines, each of which has its own tradition and which, when combined, rely on equally traditional patterns of visual perception in order to be understood and interpreted as intuitively as possible: abstract model making and virtual photography.

Of course, the interpretation of visualization presupposes a certain degree of familiarity with formal abstraction. Unlike linguistic abstraction, pictorial and especially spatial abstraction is often still subject to misunderstanding or even incomprehension. With a suitable cultural education, however, one is able to perceive abstract forms, arranged appropriately, as what they are supposed to represent. If, for example, a single vertical prism on a pentagonal base with two right angles cannot be interpreted correctly, several of these basic shapes, placed next to each other and rotated accordingly, are intuitively interpreted as a group of houses. This representation corresponds precisely to traditional model construction in architecture and urban planning and is commonly used in physical reality, from very small scales up to the scale of 1:500.

In the case of abstract geometry, in particular, it is important to refer to another architectural subdiscipline: architectural photography. Unlike photography of physical reality, where the eye is usually guided by a multitude of details to gain an idea of scale and space, abstract models often provide too few visual cues. However, if some of the conventions of traditional architectural photography are taken into account, the projection corresponds to the mental model that builds up in the viewer's imagination when walking through architecture in physical reality. In fact, human spatial perception, which takes place not only through the eyes but also through the sense of balance, usually has an unmistakable idea of which objects are vertical and which are not. Both perspectival projection, as part of descriptive geometry, and photography make it possible for vertical objects, such as lampposts, to be depicted in such a way that they appear to collapse onto each other.[6] A merely vertical image plane in the photographic composition, on the other hand, can deliberately avoid this effect and thus make it much easier for the eye to orient itself. To distinguish this projection method, which takes account of natural perception in physical reality, from the general projection of digital models, we refer to it as "virtual photography."

The following case studies are intended to illustrate the interplay between abstract model building and virtual photography for the purpose of mediation but also for the development of hypotheses based on and in the field of humanities.

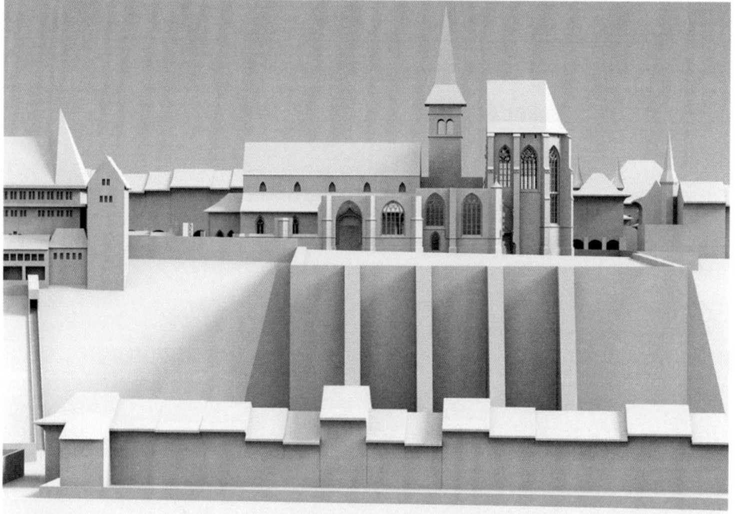

Fig. 1

Bern Cathedral

The almost fifty visualizations of scientific hypotheses in seven essays, published in the book *Das Berner Münster. Das erste Jahrhundert,*[7] are the result of the different approaches taken by the authors to their respective content [Fig. 1]. The interdisciplinary research project—which includes art history, architectural history, urban history, building research, architecture, restoration, and stonemasonry—was able to provide a picture of the hypotheses from different perspectives with the help of a virtual model [Fig. 2]. Use of the same virtual model as the spatial basis for a whole series of illustrations, which appear in their restrained sobriety in the tradition of architectural photography alongside scientific photographs of the findings, also testifies on a visual level to the close cooperation between the individual fields and their respective contributions to the creation of the compendium.

One special feature of the research findings published in *Das Berner Münster* is the hypothe-

Fig. 1 Bern Cathedral between 1438 and 1440.

Fig. 2 Bern Cathedral around 1520.

Fig. 3 Hypothetical west gallery in Bern Cathedral.

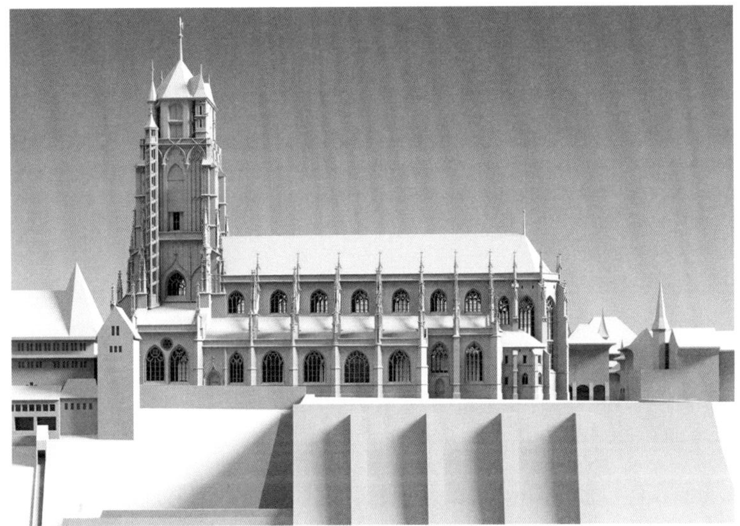

Fig. 2

sis about an originally planned inner west gallery of the Bern Cathedral; it was only fragmentarily manifested because of a change of plan. To visualize this in a way that reveals the structural consequences—but which avoids a speculative, "actual" appearance—requires abstract geometry, photographed as if it were real. Unlike the representations of hypothetical but actually implemented states, the visualization of the west gallery is the assumed form of a hypothetical state [Fig. 3]. These and other illustrated assumptions about parts of the building, components, or lost states suggest dispensing with visual information, which is regarded as uncertain or completely speculative, such as stone joints or surface structures of single stones, in favor of the ever-consistent appearance of the church over the course of its history.[8]

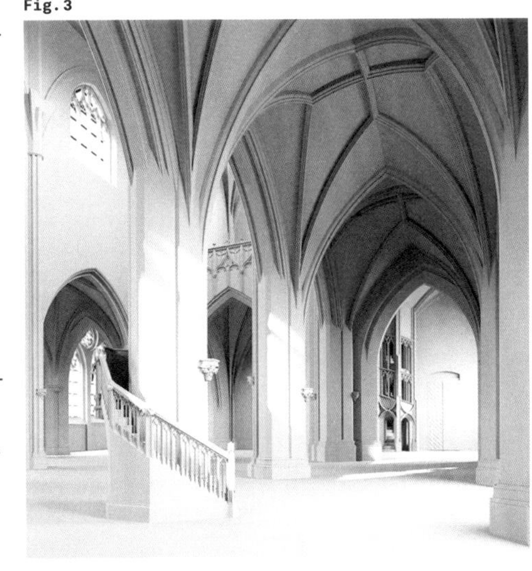

Fig. 3

Cologne Cathedral

The methodological basis for the model of Bern Cathedral, which was modeled down to the very last structural detail, was taken from the more abstract construction phases of the Cologne Cathedral and its predecessors.[9] While the Gothic building still stands today, of which the first part, the choir, was already completed in the fourteenth century, traces of the earlier buildings on the site have been lost, except for fragmentary finds and some contemporary images [Fig. 4]. The level of hypothesizing is thus much higher in the case of the Cologne Cathedral. In order to present the evolution of the churches over the course of two millennia in a comparable way, it was necessary, in this case, to dispense with showing joints and materials.

For the pre-Gothic periods, in particular, the primary architectonic focus was to assign architectural content to the findings that could not be achieved by extrapolation alone, as had

Fig. 4

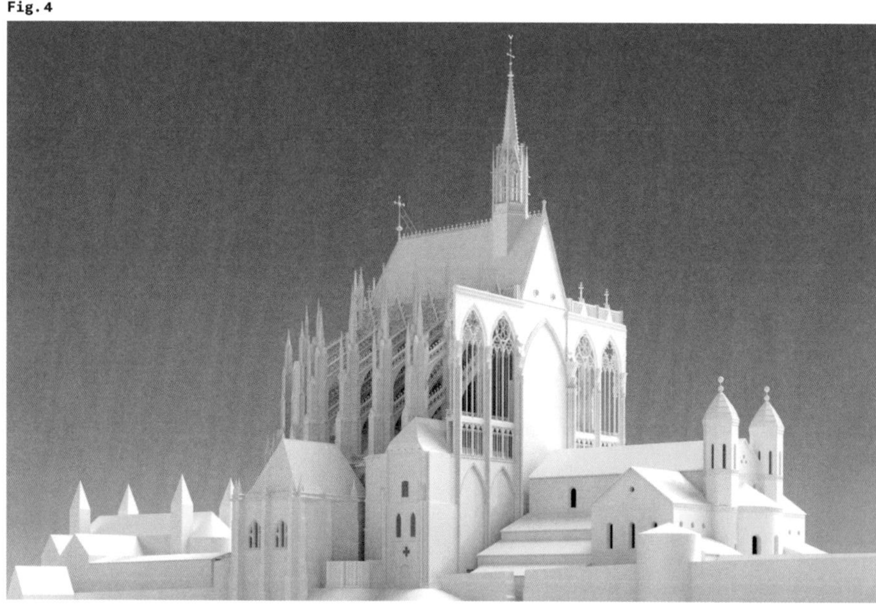

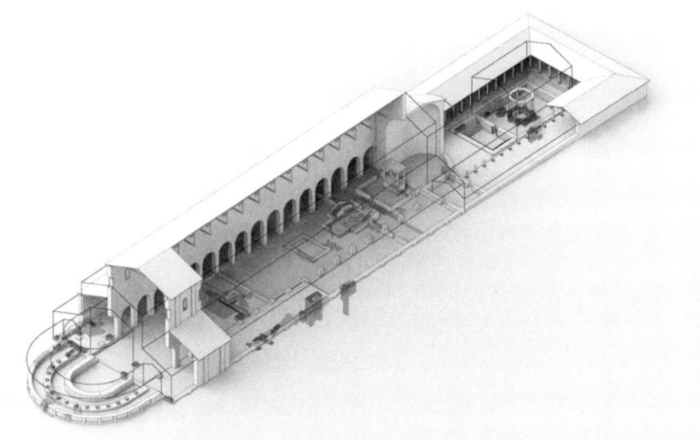

Fig. 5

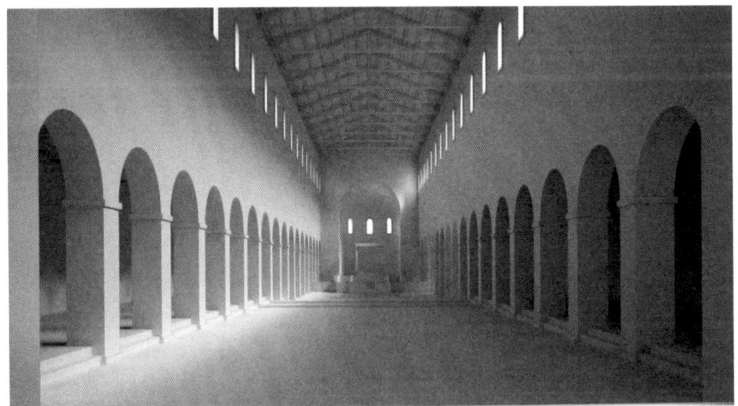

Fig. 6

been the practice in archaeology up to that point Fig. 5. These connected the individual fragments in a straight line, resulting in a possible but highly improbable appearance. However, since the actual shape can never be determined—the aforementioned test excavations excluded the possibility of future findings—the idea behind the building, which is just as likely, is presented in the form of an architectural design. This model is admittedly abstract, but it is structured, rhythmic, modular, symmetrical, and regular—in other words, just as the churches of the period would have been described in source Fig. 6.

Fig. 4 Old cathedral and gothic choir of Cologne Cathedral around 1320.

Fig. 5 Isometry of the predecessor of Cologne Cathedral in the eighth century with archaeological findings.

Fig. 6 Inside of the predecessor of Cologne Cathedral in the eighth century.

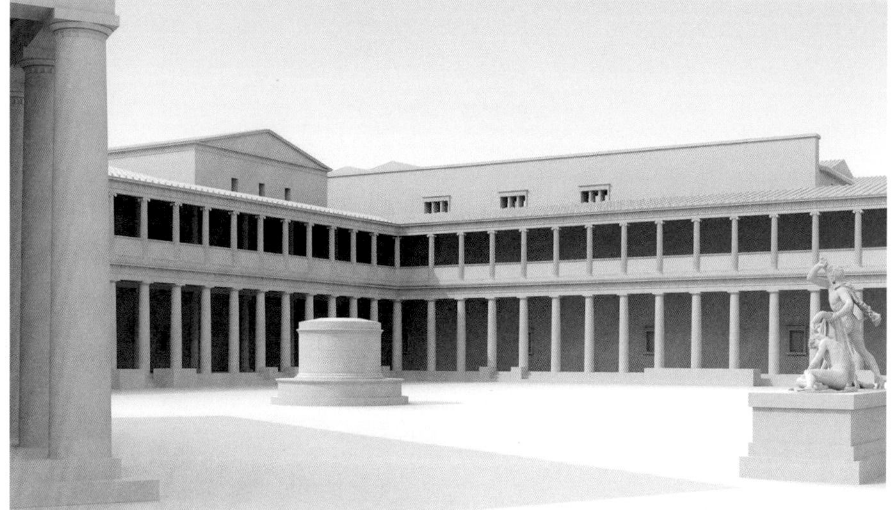

Fig. 7

Pergamon

The visualization of the ancient metropolis of Pergamon [Fig. 7] is primarily a clear evolution of the historical spatial model exhibited in the Pergamon Museum in Berlin, until its closure for renovation.[10] This shows the large building complexes—sanctuaries, markets, and gymnasiums, among others—in the middle of a park landscape of green meadows and groups of trees, similar to an English garden. In fact, however, the hill was almost completely built up on the slopes descending to the south and east.

Fig. 8

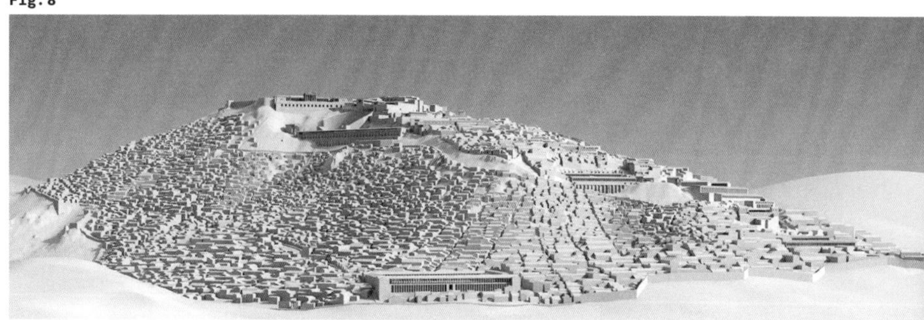

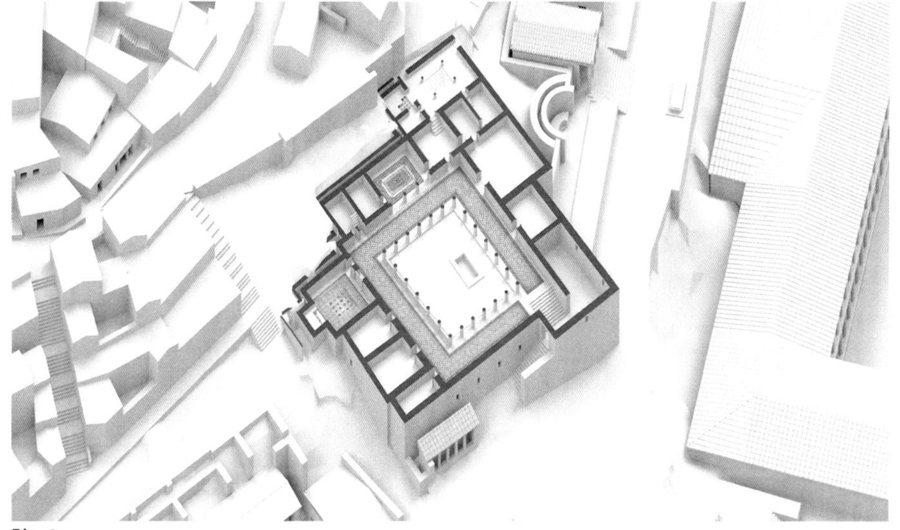

Fig. 9

Except for a few excavated sections, the individual buildings remain unknown. It has been possible to demonstrate the density of the buildings on a selective basis, aided by a general understanding of the structure of the ancient city **Fig. 8**. On the basis of these two pieces of knowledge, we have developed a city texture that makes it possible for the slopes of the mountain to be plausibly visualized as being built-up. Individual buildings are rarely more than the aforementioned pentagonal prism, but in context, the image of a city emerges in the viewer's imagination, providing the context assumed by the archaeologists for the large building complexes **Fig. 9**.

Fig. 7 Athena sanctuary in Pergamon with Ludovisi group on right.

Fig. 8 City panorama of Pergamon around 300 AD.

Fig. 9 Floor plan axonometry of building Z in Pergamon.

Ideal Church

The idea of a church that, although never implemented, was the inspiration for some three hundred parish churches built as part of a Counter-Reformation construction program in the seventeenth-century principality of Würzburg is even more hypothetical than that of the west gallery of Bern Cathedral. According to the habilitation thesis of the former cathedral master builder of Cologne Cathedral, Barbara Schock-Werner, the idea of an ideal church **Fig. 10** arose in the mind of the Würzburg Prince-Bishop Julius Echter von Mespelbrunn.[11] As with the west gallery of the Bern Cathedral, the ideal church is a meta-hypothesis. But unlike in the previous examples, in the parish churches designed according to Echter's idea, the furnishings and their interaction with the volume of the buildings are so significant that the desired result could not be achieved through the method of pure geometric abstraction for illustrating the ideal church. Therefore, the method of visualizing uncertainty had to be extended to include the method of synthesizing idealized components. Thus, during the first step, among the most important components of the completed buildings (such as the nave, choir, tower, and sacristy, of the interior and exterior color scheme) and of the furnishings

Fig. 10 Assumed ideal church by Juli[us] Echter in its ideal context.

Fig. 11 West view of the interior of t[he] ideal church.

Fig. 12 East view of the interior of th[e] ideal church.

Fig. 10

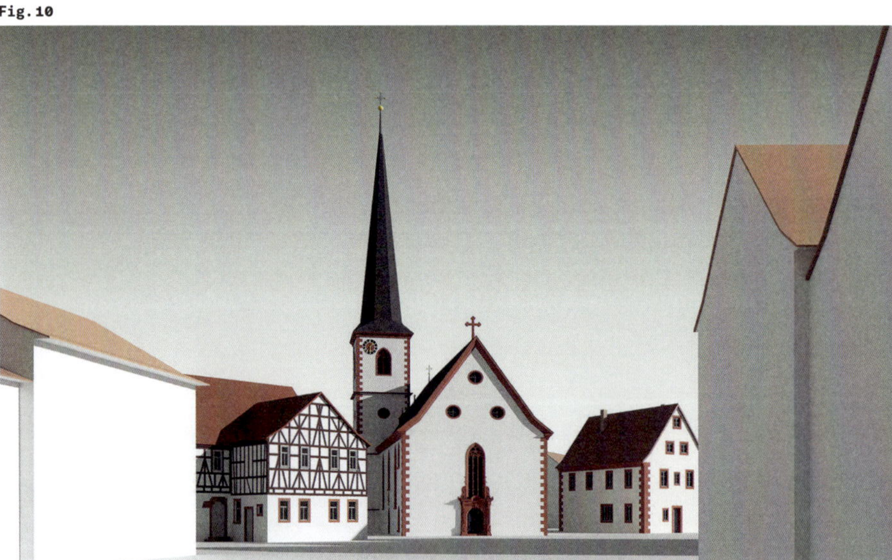

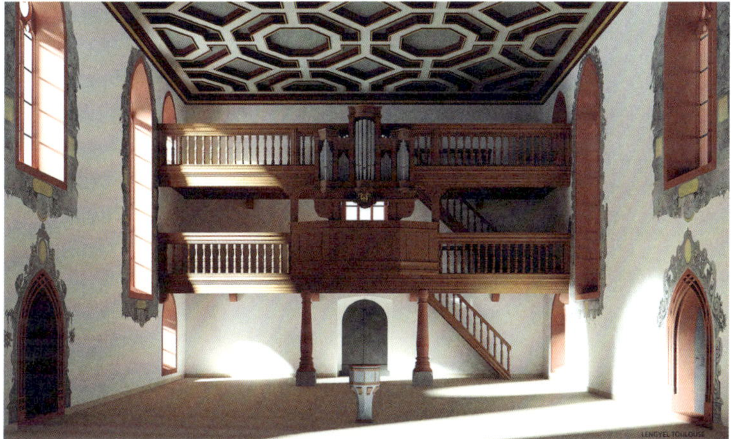

Fig. 11

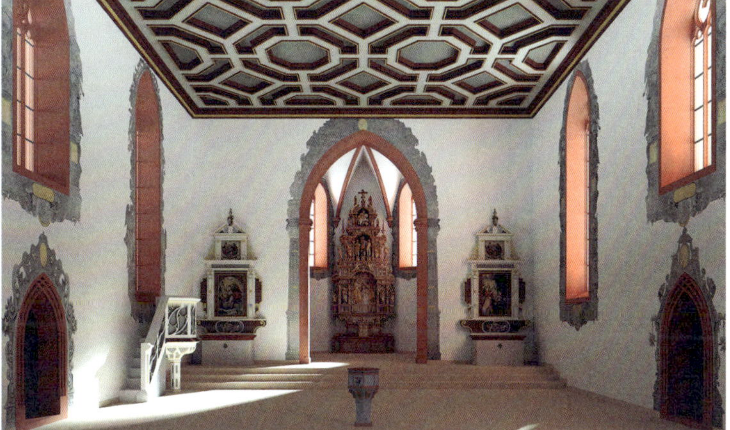

Fig. 12

(such as altars, gallery, pulpit, and baptismal font), one was identified as the most typical out of the multitude of actual variants ^{Fig. 11}. Following subsequent adjustments to the dimensions and formal detail modeling, these were combined, primarily using symmetries, modules, and dimensions. The result was a spatial collage, which, however, does not reveal its composition of different parts, since the elements are fully integrated ^{Fig. 12}. Only knowledge of each individual church from which the set pieces were borrowed discloses the collage method. The signature of Echter is nevertheless immediately recognizable and obvious.[12]

The visualization of lost buildings or building states through virtual models remains an important method for archaeology, art history, and the—also digital— mediation of cultural assets in museums and exhibitions. Instead of speculative details, the abstraction in the visualization enables the viewer to focus on the underlying idea of the building. //

[1] As part of the German Research Foundation's priority program DFG-SPP 2172 "The Digital Image," the authors from the Department of Architecture and Visualization at Brandenburgische Technische Universität Cottbus-Senftenberg (BTU), together with the Kunstgeschichtliches Institut of the Philipps-Universität Marburg, use a research project entitled "Architecture Transformed—Architectural Processes in the Digital Image Space" to show, among other things, how new media in architectural representations developed between 1980 and 2020; this work is based on research into trade journals and a competition involving students and young architects.

[2] Such programs, known as art generators, have different focal points; examples include Midjourney (see https://alternativeto.net/software/midjourney/about/) and DALL-E (see https://openai.com), basically the visual equivalent of ChatGPT.

[3] The term *reality* is controversial. The debate on realism will not be addressed here, however. Rather, it is about the mere difference between objects, which are undoubtedly part of our environment, and ideas, to which initially no visible or tangible form can be attributed.

[4] Even the term *medium* is not used uniformly. This is already shown by the term *new media*, which is predominantly limited to technical, if not exclusively digital, sound, image, and film formats.

[5] Located at Kämpchensweg 58 in a Cologne residential suburb, the building was constructed between 1994 and 1996 according to plans by architect Oswald Mathias Ungers as his third private residence. See *Bauten und Projekte 1991–1998* (Milan and Stuttgart: Electa and Deutsche Verlags-Anstalt, 1998), 339, no. 248: Haus Ungers 3.

[6] Descriptive geometry is one of the subjects taught at the Department of Architecture and Visualization at BTU.

[7] Bernd Nicolai and Jürg Schweizer, eds., *Das Berner Münster. Das erste Jahrhundert: Von der Grundsteinlegung bis zur Chorvollendung und Reformation (1421–1517/1528)* (Regensburg: Schnell & Steiner, 2019).

[8] A detailed description of the method—in particular, the balancing of the abstraction of form, contour, jointing, and materiality—can be found in the authors' relevant contribution in the book on the Bern Cathedral. See Dominik Lengyel and Catherine Toulouse, "Zum Erscheinungsbild der Visualisierungen des Berner Münsters," in *Das Berner Münster*, eds. Nicolai and Schweizer, 218–30.

[9] In addition to a film shown on-site since 2010 in the entrance area to the archaeological zone and the ascent of the west towers, the authors have published a book on the construction phases of the Cologne Cathedral and its predecessor buildings together with the former cathedral master builder. See Barbara Schock-Werner, Dominik Lengyel, and Catherine Toulouse, eds., *Die Bauphasen des Kölner Domes und seiner Vorgängerbauten / Cologne Cathedral and preceding buildings* (Cologne: Kölner Domverlag, 2011).

[10] In the exhibition catalog, the authors, together with the archaeologists directly involved, describe the creation of the first complete scientific model of the city-mountain of Pergamon. See Eric Laufer et al., "Die Wiederentstehung Pergamons als virtuelles Stadtmodell," in *Pergamon. Panorama der antiken Metropole: Begleitbuch zur Ausstellung,* ed. Ralf Grüssinger, Volker Kästner, and Andreas Scholl, 2nd ed. (Petersberg: Michael Imhof, 2012), 82–86.

[11] Barbara Schock-Werner, "Bauen in der Fläche. Echters Baupolitik im Hochstift," in *Julius Echter. Patron der Künste: Konturen eines Fürsten und Bischofs der Renaissance*, ed. Damian Dombrowski, Markus Josef Maier, and Fabian Müller (Berlin: Deutscher Kunstverlag, 2017), 115–26 and 130–34.

[12] Related articles on Julius Echter's architecture as well as on the method of visualizing his hypothetical ideal church can be found in the exhibition catalog Schock-Werner, "Bauen in der Fläche," 115–26 and 130–34; see also Dominik Lengyel and Catherine Toulouse, "Die Echtersche Idealkirche. Eine interaktive Annäherung," in Dombrowski, Josef, and Müller, *Julius Echter. Patron der Künste*, 127–29.

BIOGRAPHIES

Keyvane Alinaghi

is an artist and developer based in Lille. He exhibits and performs internationally. He promotes a do-it-yourself and open-source practice of computer code and proposes methods of valorization and sharing of technical tools for designers and musicians. He teaches creative code at the Ecole Supérieure d'Art et de Communication de Cambrai.

Sarah Amsler

worked as an information specialist at various GLAM institutions in Switzerland. At SARI, she coordinated the Swiss Art and Architecture Thesaurus® (AAT®) Translation Initiative. She is interested in the valorization of cultural heritage through digitization strategies.

Régine Bonnefoit

holds a doctorate in art history (University of Heidelberg, 1995) and has obtained her habilitation (University of Passau, 2006). She won a research grant at the Institute of Art History in Florence (1995–98). Between 2001 and 2006, she was a university assistant at the University of Lausanne. After a professorship at the Swiss National Science Foundation (SNSF), she was appointed full professor at the University of Neuchâtel. She is the curator of numerous exhibitions.

Katharina Brandl

is head of the division of visual arts at the Swiss arts council Pro Helvetia and was artistic director of Kunstraum Niederoesterreich in Vienna from 2019 to 2022. By training, she is a political scientist and art historian, focusing on the history of contemporary art.

Fleur Chevalier

holds a doctorate in aesthetics, science, and technology of the arts. In 2020, she defended her PhD thesis on the history of videographic and cathodic practices on French television, entitled "Formater pour mieux régner: vidéastes et performeurs à l'épreuve de la télédistribution en France, 1975–1998" (Formatting to better reign: video artists and performers confronting TV distribution in France, 1975–1998).

Aline Guillermet

focuses on the impact of digital technologies on artistic practices since the 1960s. Selected publications include "Vera Molnar's Computer Paintings" (*Representations*, 2020) and *Gerhard Richter and the Technological Condition of Painting* (Edinburgh University Press, 2024).

Thomas Hänsli

is director of the Swiss Art Research Infrastructure (SARI, University of Zurich) and director of gta Digital (ETH Zurich). He has a background in architectural history. His fields of research are in early modern art and architecture, the theory of architecture, and digital research methods.

Dominik Lengyel

is chair of architecture and visualization at Brandenburgische Technische Universität. He worked as an architect at Prof. O. M.

Ungers and has an architecture firm, cofounded with Catherine Toulouse. He is a member of the European Academy of Sciences and Arts in Salzburg. He has received funding from DFG (German Research Foundation), DAI, Gerda Henkel Foundation, and German Federal Ministries BMBF, BMWi, and BMI.

Melissa Rérat

is a postdoctoral researcher at the University of Applied Arts Vienna (fellow of the Swiss National Science Foundation [SNSF]). Previously, she was a scientific collaborator at the Swiss Institute for Art Research (SIK-ISEA) and taught the history of new media at the University of Neuchâtel. Her doctoral thesis (2020, published in 2022) studied the social construction of video art through discourse in the 1970s.

Samuel Schellenberg

holds a master's degree in art history, history, and English from the University of Lausanne (1998). Since 2008, he has been in charge of the cultural section of the newspaper *Le Courrier*, based in Geneva. In 2019, he was winner of the Prix Meret Oppenheim—the Swiss Grand Award for Art created in 2001 by the Federal Office of Culture and the Federal Art Commission.

Catherine Toulouse

is an assistant professor of architecture and visualization at Brandenburgische Technische Universität. She worked in the office of the architect Prof. O. M. Ungers and later cofounded an architecture firm with Dominik Lengyel. Clients include Cologne Cathedral, Bern Minster Foundation, Egyptian Museum Munich, Martin v. Wagner Museum Würzburg, and Insurance Association BGRCI, among others.

Caroline Tron-Carroz

holds a doctorate in art history and teaches at the Ecole Supérieure d'Art et de Communication de Cambrai. She is a full member of the InTRu laboratory at the University of Tours and contributes to the editorial board of the journal *exPosition*. Her research focuses on the television object and electronic experimentations in the field of art.

Zsofi Valyi-Nagy

is a postdoctoral fellow at the Getty Research Institute, Los Angeles, CA. She earned her doctorate in art history from the University of Chicago in 2023. Her work has received support from the Dedalus Foundation, the Fulbright Program, the DAAD (German Academic Exchange Service), and the National Gallery of Art in Washington, DC.

Nina Zschocke

is a researcher and lecturer in contemporary art history and media theory at the Institute for the History and Theory of Architecture gta, ETH Zurich. She holds a PhD from the University of Cologne and has been a postdoc at the Institute of Art History at University Zurich, a DFG (Deutsche Forschungsgemeinschaft) research fellow, and the scientific coordinator of two doctoral programs.

INDEX

PHOTO CREDITS

Article Zsofi Valyi-Nagy

Fig. 1 © Szöllősi-Nagy–Nemes Collection, Hungary; photo by Péter Herendi

Fig. 2 © Vera Molnar archives, used with the artist's permission, photographer unknown

Fig. 3 © Szöllősi-Nagy–Nemes Collection, Hungary; photo by Zsofi Valyi-Nagy

Article Katharina Brandl

Figs. 1-2 © Joseph DeLappe

Article Aline Guillermet

Fig. 1 © Erica Scourti 2023, courtesy of the artist

Fig. 2 © Jonas Lund 2023, courtesy of the artist; photo: Michel Boulogne

Fig. 3 reproduced with the authors' permission; Ranjay Krishna, Yuke Zhu et al., "Visual Genome: Connecting Language and Vision Using Crowdsourced Dense Image Annotations," *International Journal of Computer Vision* 123, no. 1 (2017): 32–73, here 35.

Figs. 4-5 © Toby Ziegler 2023, courtesy of the artist

Article Nina Zschocke

Fig. 1 © Rory Pilgrim

Fig. 2 courtesy andriesse eyck galerie

Fig. 3 photo: Tim Klauser

Fig. 4 © U5

pp. 82-85 © U5

Article Keyvane Alinaghi and Caroline Tron-Carroz

Figs. 1-3 © ESAC Cambrai

Article Dominik Lengyel and Catherine Toulouse

Figs. 1-12 © Lengyel Toulouse Architects Berlin

Régine Bonnefoit, Melissa Rérat, and Samuel Schellenberg (Eds.)

Keyvane Alinaghi and Caroline Tron-Carroz, Sarah Amsler and Thomas Hänsli, Katharina Brandl, Fleur Chevalier, Aline Guillermet, Catherine Toulouse and Dominik Lengyel, Zsofi Valyi-Nagy, Nina Zschocke (authors)

Swiss Association of Art Historians (VKKS-ASHHA-ASSSA), Pavillonweg 2, 3012 Bern, Switzerland, www.vkks.ch

V Vereinigung der Kunsthistorikerinnen und Kunsthistoriker in der Schweiz

Association suisse des historiennes et historiens de l'art

Associazione svizzera delle storiche e degli storici dell'arte

Printed with the financial support of the Swiss Association of Art Historians, Articulations (Swiss Association for Young Art Historians), and the Institute of Art History and Museum Studies at the University of Neuchâtel.

Articulations
Association suisse pour la relève en histoire de l'art
Schweizer Verein für den kunsthistorischen Nachwuchs

Concept Régine Bonnefoit, Melissa Rérat, Samuel Schellenberg, and the Swiss Association of Art Historians

Content and Production Editor Katharina Holas, Birkhäuser Verlag, Vienna, Austria

Translation from German/French and proofreading Scribe Ltd., Biel/Bienne, Switzerland

Copyediting/Proofreading Elizabeth H. Stern, Heidelberg, Germany

Layout/cover design/typography Kathleen Bernsdorf, Berlin, Germany

Image editing Pixelstorm Litho & Digital Imaging, Vienna, Austria

Printing Beltz Grafische Betriebe GmbH, Bad Langensalza, Germany

Paper Lona Offset FSC 120 gsm, Surbalin smooth 115 gsm, Maxigloss 135 gsm

Typeface Moderat, Source Serif Pro

Library of Congress Control Number: 2022951358

Bibliographic information published by the German National Library

The German National Library lists this publication in the Deutsche Nationalbibliografie; detailed bibliographic data are available on the Internet at http://dnb.dnb.de.

ISBN 978-3-11-118592-7
e-ISBN (PDF) 978-3-11-118600-9

© 2023 Walter de Gruyter GmbH, Berlin/ Boston

www.degruyter.com

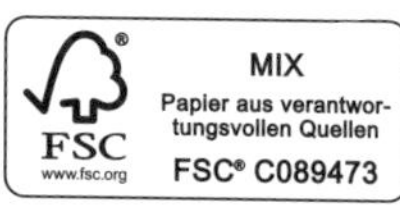